"YELLOWSTONE KELLY"

"YELLOWSTONE KELLY"

IN 1878

"Yellowstone Kelly"

The Memoirs of Luther S. Kelly

EDITED BY M. M. QUAIFE

WITH A FOREWORD BY
LIEUTENANT-GENERAL NELSON A. MILES, U. S. A.

UNIVERSITY OF NEBRASKA PRESS
LINCOLN AND LONDON

Copyright, 1926, by Yale University Press

Printed in the United States of America

Library of Congress Catalog Card Number 26–9001

International Standard Book Number 0–8032–5784–8

~ *First Bison Book printing: August 1973*

Most recent printing shown by the first digit below:

4   5   6   7   8   9   10

Bison Book edition reproduced by arrangement
with the Yale University Press.

HISTORICAL INTRODUCTION

TO Americans of whatever generation the land of opportunity and of adventure has always lain along the western frontier of settlement and civilization. Today, the frontier has disappeared from America and the process of idealizing it in myth and romance has long since begun. With sure commercial instinct for that which appeals most powerfully to the public, the moving picture industry has exploited unceasingly the theme of the frontier, and in the world of the silver screen the "western" disputes with the eternal theme of romantic love for primacy in the hearts of the multitude. Nor does this popular estimate of the importance which attaches to the subject of frontier life and adventure differ materially from the judgment of scholarship. For a generation the historians have been engaged in exploiting the story of the frontier in American history, and there is today practically unanimous acceptance, among scholars, of the view with which the career of Professor Turner is so intimately bound up, that to the existence and influence of the frontier we owe those things which chiefly distinguish American institutions and character from those of the Old World.

In the narrative of "Yellowstone Kelly" we have a rare story of adventure and service. General Miles, who knew him long and intimately, fitly compares him with such heroes of the American wilderness as Daniel Boone and David Crockett. We think of these men as the products of a bygone age and environment, as indeed they were. Yet Mr. Kelly still lives in his California home, a

Historical Introduction

witness of the mechanical marvels and the material progress which mark the third decade of the twentieth century. Like Boone, he is a lover of solitude and of the wilderness; unlike Boone, he has had the desire to preserve for posterity the story of the life he loved, and the education and literary capacity requisite to the task. His story is at once an important contribution to the history of the western frontier in the decades to which it pertains and a thrilling tale of sustained adventure whose perusal should bring delight to every normal man or boy.

In editing the narrative my principal task has been one of condensation. The manuscript as originally prepared by Mr. Kelly was much longer than the contents of the present volume. In preparing it for the press I have freely altered the construction of sentences and paragraphs, and have deleted unessential details. But the story, as printed, remains the author's own; his are the ideas and the statements of fact or opinion, and his also the manner of expressing them, which seems to me in essence profoundly poetic.

M. M. QUAIFE

Burton Historical Collection,
    Detroit.

CONTENTS

ILLUSTRATIONS

FOREWORD

DURING the transformation of the Great West from wild prairies and mountain waste to peaceful settled communities and states, a series of wars occurred between the white race and the hostile Indians in which very conspicuous and heroic characters appeared. At that time that vast country was roamed over by strong tribes of hostile Indians, and millions of buffalo, wild horses, bear, wolves, elk, antelope, and deer.

The nomadic Indians in time had to give place to the home-builders, who developed the vast treasures of agricultural and mineral wealth that have made our republic prosperous and great. Now the railroads and telegraph lines have taken the place of the Indian trails, and millions of domestic stock have replaced the wild beasts. The music of peace and happiness is now heard where the tom-tom and the battle cry were formerly the signal for savage warfare.

During that exciting and eventful period there appeared a most interesting character, equally as fearless, intelligent, and resourceful as Daniel Boone, David Crockett, Kit Carson, or William F. Cody. His name was Luther S. Kelly but he was better known as "Yellowstone Kelly." He loved the romance of the frontier and seemed to appreciate and enjoy the beauty and grandeur of nature in the highest degree. "Yellowstone Kelly" was of good family, well educated and fond of good books, as quiet and gentle as he was brave, as kind and generous as he was forceful, a great hunter and an

Foreword

expert rifleman; he explored that extensive northwest country years before serious hostilities occurred and acquired a knowledge of its topography, climate, and resources that was exceedingly valuable.

My first acquaintance with "Yellowstone Kelly" was when campaigning against hostile Indians in Montana, North Dakota, and Wyoming. He came from the valley of the Yellowstone entirely alone to my camp on the banks of that river, near the mouth of the Tongue River. He had recently killed a large bear and cut off one of its huge paws, and upon this he inscribed his name and sent it to my tent, as he had no cards at the time! In return I sent for him, and found him a most interesting character and soon engaged his services. At that time he was young and strong, a fine horseman, as supple as a panther, with an eye like the eagle. His knowledge of that unmapped region was most valuable, and as a guide and leader of the scouts and advance guard he was exceedingly useful. His knowledge of the Indians, their habits, and hunting grounds was always reliable.

During the series of campaigns against the hostile Indian tribes, the Hunkpapa, Miniconjou, Sans Arcs, Oglala, Cheyenne, Nez Percés, and Bannock under such noted warriors as Sitting Bull, Crazy Horse, Two Moons, Spotted Eagle, White Bull, Lame Deer, and Chief Joseph (whose Indian name was "Thunder Moving over the Mountains"), "Yellowstone Kelly" was exceedingly enterprising, reliable, and fearless, always and under all circumstances representing the highest type of the true American spirit and character.

Later he became an officer and rendered distinguished and valuable services in Alaska and the Philippine Is-

Foreword

lands. A hero in war, a true American patriot in times of peace, it gives me pleasure to commend him and his adventurous story to those who are interested in the history of what was formerly the frontier of our beloved country.

NELSON A. MILES,
Lieutenant-General, U.S.A.

Washington, March 1, 1921.

"YELLOWSTONE KELLY"

CHAPTER I

MY YEARS IN THE ARMY

I FIRST saw the light among the wonderful Finger Lakes of central New York, in the historic region made famous by Red Jacket and other noted chiefs of the Iroquois confederacy. If the legend be true, these lakes were formed when the Great Spirit dropped here a slice of the happy hunting grounds and left the imprint of his fingers in the soft rocks so that his chosen people, the Iroquois, could ply their bark canoes in deep waters and build their habitations on the shores of secluded lakes.

Along Seneca Lake and the deep woods that bordered it I passed many a happy day of my boyhood, encroaching, no doubt, upon many hours that should have been devoted to school. The inclination I had for forest life and scenes, and later for the free life of the plains and mountains of the Far West, may have been derived from ancestry, for my family claims descent from that strong character of early New England days, Hannah Dustin, who, having been captured by Indians, rose stealthily in the night when all were asleep, and killing several of her captors, finally reached her home and friends after an exhausting journey through swamps and forests.

The opening steps in the Civil War, culminating in the attack on Fort Sumter in April, 1861, came with a series of shocks to my native village of Geneva, and the excitement that prevailed is still fresh in my memory.

1

"Yellowstone Kelly"

There was marching by night of "Little Giants" and "Lincoln Clubs" in resolute and solemn array, and I yet recall how the oil dripped down from dusky, smoky torches onto black wide-awakes and capes. Many of those who so gaily or solemnly passed marched later in lines of battle, and came back from the war battered or crippled, or came not at all.

Nearly everybody wore a rosette of red, white, and blue, and some of these were very gorgeous indeed. A regiment of volunteers was soon recruited and a training camp was established in the outskirts of the village. I well remember the day when the regiment, fully equipped for service, marched down Main Street before my entranced eyes to the music of a line of drummer boys stepping in front, among whom, to my astonishment, I saw two or three of my schoolfellows. This set me to thinking deeply and I deplored the fact that my youth and my position as eldest in the family rendered it imperative that I remain with my mother, sister, and brothers.

Toward the close of the war, having obtained my mother's consent, I left the academy at Lima, New York, where I had been attending school, to enlist as a soldier. I was then not yet sixteen years of age. I have a dim recollection of going before a board of officials in my native village, who, after an examination, directed me to proceed to Rochester, where I would have the opportunity I desired to join the army.

On reaching Rochester I presented myself to the recruiting officer for the Fourth New York Cavalry, but was summarily rejected because of my youth. Made wise by this first failure—although at that period I had not heard of the young recruit who, having been rejected in his first effort to enlist, rushed over to a shoe store, had himself fitted to a pair of shoes, and ordered that they be marked number eighteen, so that he could say he was *over* eighteen—I succeeded in my second attempt. The regular army officer who examined me on this occasion seemed impressed by my good looks and tall stature. I was enrolled in the regular establishment, and shortly a sergeant took me in charge and furnished me a suit of army blue, which I donned with much satisfaction. So green was I at this time that I did not know the difference between the volunteer and the regular army.

Passing over trivial incidents, such as being served with coffee without milk and bread without butter, I soon found myself en route for New York. For a few days we were housed with other recruits in a curious, circular structure called Castle William, which stood on the point of Governors Island nearest the Battery, when we were ordered aboard a transport bound for City Point, Virginia. I have little recollection of our voyage except that it was a misty and boisterous one. Coffee, hard-tack, and meat were served out to us on the forward, unprotected deck of the ship, and I did not see an officer until we arrived at City Point.

Here, all was confusion. A multitude of tugs and steamers enlivened the water-side, while officers and soldiers rushed about on shore amid a lot of military wagons, tents, and other equipment. Disembarking, we were marched a short distance to a camp and there lined up for assignment to certain skeleton companies, whose ranks had been depleted by losses suffered in recent service. We were then issued equipment and dismissed.

My captain proved to be a stout, cocky fellow who

had evidently been promoted from the ranks. He was, however, an efficient officer. "Bring down those hands with vim," was a favorite order when on drill. For some time our service consisted in guarding prisoners of war, and also general prisoners in bull pens.

After the cessation of hostilities, we marched from Burkesville to Richmond, the view of which was marred by burned buildings and bridges. Later we took the road to Washington. At no time had I met more than one battalion of my regiment. Our battalion was commanded by Captain Robert Hall, and Lieutenant Theodore Schwan was adjutant. When next I met these officers, a third of a century later, one was in the adjutant general's office in Washington, and the other was in the Philippines, and both were brigadier generals.

Arrived in Washington, the battalion encamped south of the Potomac in the pines, where we remained until after the Grand Review. On the evening of June 6, 1865, I was detailed as one of fifty men to act as guard on the following day near the reviewing officer, on the occasion of the review of the Sixth Army Corps. Long before daybreak we were on the road marching through the misty, fog-covered stretches to the Potomac. On either side, as we passed, could be heard the morning call of bugle, fife, and drum, and stentorian voices giving commands to moving cavalry.

Finally, in the morning light we saw the Potomac and the low land about it. We crossed the historic Long Bridge, and at length stopped to rest at some point on Pennsylvania Avenue. Here, I remember, I purchased a small pie of a negress, who had a stand near by. The pie looked fine, but when tested it proved to be thin and tough. The crust was not of the kind that melts in the

LUTHER S. KELLY

As a Private, Company G, 10th Infantry, April, 1865.

From a Daguerreotype.

mouth, and I retired disappointed and hungry; the soiled shin-plaster which I paid for it was wasted.

About ten o'clock the officer in command lined us up in front of the reviewing stand. As yet no one was at hand to occupy the vast structure, which rose tier upon tier of rough boarding, gaily decorated with flags and bunting, although crowds of holiday sightseers were beginning to throng the streets. We were soon ordered to stand at ease, and it was a relief to look about and compare notes.

Presently squads of police came along and stationed men at intervals to clear the way. Our detachment was brought to attention, for the column could be seen in the distance moving down the avenue. By this time the reviewing stand was filling rapidly through the different entrances; generals and staff and field officers were much in evidence, while members of Congress and others prominent in official and civil life were being frequently greeted with bursts of cheers.

Soon all was excitement, as a burst of music heralded the approach of a column of mounted police who led the way, followed, as I recall, by an escort of cavalry. Close on their heels came the commander of the Sixth Corps and his staff, followed by orderlies, the corps headquarters guards, and bands; then came the first division with its staff, followed by columns of troops passing in review in lines of companies, the left of the line being only a few yards away from where we were. As the heads of the different organizations passed along we stood at "present arms" until our fingers and arms ached with the tension. Bronze-bearded fellows they were, clad in the blue field uniform of blouse and cap or black hat; infantry, cavalry, and artillery marched with the precision and compelling force of veterans—a latent power that enemies of the Republic might well have taken note of.

I was but a recruit, and was unable to identify any of the famous warriors who moved so gallantly by, but I noted one dashing officer of high rank whose horse seemed to have gotten the bit and was bearing his rider at full speed along the line of march before he could curb him. It may have been Custer of the waving locks, although I am not sure.

All day long that column passed, and our arms became numb with saluting and holding our rifles at a carry. Some regiments were arrayed in white collars and many had new uniforms; other regiments, perhaps direct from the field, had had no time to make requisitions on the quartermaster for new clothing. So they passed, horse, foot, and artillery, followed by camp followers and "bummers" in strange and quaint attire gathered in foraging forays on the flanks of armies.

After our battalion had been encamped for some time at Kalorama Heights my company was sent into Washington and stationed in some old quarters, where we suffered a good deal of discomfort from the heat and the unsavory conditions generally. At length word came that our regiment was to move to the Northwest to take station on the frontier. Presently, after considerable preparation, we boarded some antiquated day-coaches and began our journey. Of it I remember little save an incident at one station where iron kettles of hot coffee, sweetened with molasses, were brought into the car and with this, together with hard-tack and slices of pork, our hunger was satisfied.

Arrived at St. Paul, my company and one other were

assigned to Fort Ripley on the upper reaches of the Mississippi River, and shortly after we took up the line of march through a thinly settled region to that point. There was little excitement at this post and when winter set in the routine of duty was dreary enough, but in the spring, when the genial sun transformed the dead verdure into a blanket of green, I joyed in taking my rifle and rambling through the silent forests and along the pebbly banks of the Mississippi and its tributary streams.

When spring had advanced somewhat, the company received orders to march across country and take station at Fort Wadsworth, Dakota Territory, in the vicinity of Big Stone Lake. The country was still but sparsely settled and in our march we encountered but few towns or villages, so that it was not uncommon to see deer break away from the head of the column. Whenever this occurred the captain would direct two of our best shots, who were usually veteran soldiers, to go ahead and kill them. I noticed, however, that they seldom brought in any meat. We came upon numerous lakes, and our camp was usually pitched on the bank of one of them. Here I was in my element, for I was an expert swimmer, and I rather astonished the officers and men by my long underwater dashes.

Finally, my chance came. We made an early camp, and after the tents were pitched I walked to the captain's tent, saluted, and asked permission to go hunting.

"Have you had any experience in hunting?" he inquired.

"No, sir," I replied, "but I do not see any of the expert hunters bringing in game, and I would like to try my hand."

7

He smiled, and gave me the required permission, warning me at the same time not to get lost.

I had noted, a mile back on the road as we came along, an open glade crossing a water course. I reached this opening through the woods and skirted the timber along it for some distance and then, striking a game trail at right angles, turned off on it, but left it again as I touched trails leading in the direction of the opening. Once I caught sight of two white flags and saw the deer as they took a long leap together over some tall brush. I now became more wary. It was getting on toward evening and I finally retraced my steps in the direction of camp after missing two good shots because I was not ready. At length I stopped in a trail to listen, and seemed to hear the muffled sound of chopping in the direction of the camp. While thus engaged I caught the sound of light hoofs pounding the ground and suddenly in the path a buck appeared, coming full tilt directly toward me. As I raised my gun I inadvertently called out "whoa"; he stopped short as I fired low on his neck, bringing him to the ground.

He was too heavy for me to pack or drag as he was, and I was glad that no one was around to see the awkward way in which I opened him with my pocket-knife and rid him of entrails and blood. He was still too heavy to pack, so I let him drain and scraped the blood from his coat; then, with much difficulty I cut off his head as near the ears as possible.

I knew how to pack a deer, for I had seen the process. I cut through the second joints of the front feet to the muscles, then slipped my knife down between the bone and muscles to the hoof joint. By inserting these bones through the thin part of the hind legs a lock is made to swing over the shoulder. I carried the deer in this fashion and my entry into camp was spectacular. I held a reception with all the honors. After the carcass had been duly inspected I was directed to turn it over to the company cook.

Our route now led direct toward the foothills of the Coteau des Prairies. We were leaving the timbered lake country of western Minnesota and entering the region of the great plains. There was a tang in the air and the very herbage was odorous of the range that attracts wild game.

Soon we came in view of Big Stone Lake, with Lake Traverse near by, with the Browns' homestead looming like a gem amid its background of green hills. Lake Traverse, I was told, is the source of the Red River of the North, which runs very straight to Hudson Bay, while the waters of Big Stone Lake flow in the opposite direction, toward the Mississippi.

At our noon camp in the foothills a troop of Minnesota volunteer cavalry passed by in irregular column. Impatient to regain their homes after dreary service in the Dakota foothills, they would not wait for any formal turning over of the garrison, but skipped out bag and baggage, leaving a quartermaster to attend to the details. They were a soldierly-looking lot of men, and though roughly clad and mounted seemed fit for service in the field. Under their slouched black hats they took in "us regulars" as merely Uncle Sam's unit to form their relief. I should have liked much to talk with them and gain some knowledge of the life and country ahead of us.

Later in the day we rounded the point of a hill and beheld the long-looked-for Fort Wadsworth, nestling between two small lakes and surrounded by a mere embankment of earth. We soon marched in and were assigned to one of the company quarters which had been vacated by our Minnesota friends.

Fort Wadsworth belonged to the usual type of frontier post, having a square parade ground surrounded on one side by a set of officers' quarters and offices, with log quarters for three companies of troops and stables and corrals completing the other sides of a square. The aspect it presented was cheerless enough, with not a tree nor a foot of cultivated ground.

The nearest post to the westward was at Devil's Lake, but there was not a settlement anywhere in the country nearer than those we had left behind in Minnesota. The region was devoid of both Indians and big game, other than a few white-tail deer in the sparse timber of the adjacent foothills.

Early in the autumn the captain of my company, who was also quartermaster and commissary, sent for me and said: "Corporal, you will take three six-mule teams and wagons and proceed to Sauk Center, Minnesota, and load with potatoes and other vegetables and return to this post. You will be furnished a saddle horse and carbine, and besides the three drivers the post interpreter will accompany your party as guide. You will allow no other person to join your party."

I felt quite elated a day or two later, a tall, half-breed Sioux guide alongside, as I rode down the trail in the lead of my small wagon train, with my letter of instructions in my pocket. I was only a boy, and so I felt rather proud of the responsibility of my first command. When we were about ready to halt for our camp the first night we were joined by a sergeant of one of the other companies, who had been sent by his captain to purchase supplies for the company. I informed him of my instructions.

"Oh, well," he said, "I am not a person; I am a full-fledged non-commissioned officer like yourself. Of course, if you insist upon a strict interpretation of your orders I will walk ahead or behind your command and thus meet requirements."

I did not insist on this, and I was glad to have his company for he proved to be a good fellow. He rode in one of the empty wagons and I did not envy him for I well know what a comfortless vehicle a springless heavy army wagon is.

The guide spoke a little English, and being familiar with the region, pointed out to us various spots of interest, among them the ruins of a burned stockade where the Minnesota Sioux had put to death some settlers who had gathered there for mutual protection during the uprising of 1862.

We camped one night near Lake Amelia, just about dusk. Seeing a farmhouse on the opposite side of the lake, the guide and I rode around to it to see if we could get some milk and fresh vegetables. We found the door open and a fire burning in the stove, but no one was in sight or hearing and we were obliged to return empty-handed. The family may have been visiting some neighbor or it may have fled at the approach of an Indian, garbed in blanket, shirt, and leggings.

Next day we started very early and before sunrise saw two elk jump over a farmer's fence and scurry into thick timber. Finally, we entered Sauk Center, then a straggling village of one street, and passed on a couple of miles to a farm where we were to load our wagons with potatoes, onions, and turnips for the return journey. We lay over there for several days, as the farmer was away. The people were very friendly and invited me to their table, which I thoroughly enjoyed after living on hard-tack, bacon, and such fresh meat as we could pick up on the trip.

In 1866 Sauk Center was a very small village in the midst of a farming section. The sergeant camped there with some German acquaintances and invited me to come up and stay overnight. I found them most agreeable people and the table I sat down to that evening was something to remember, loaded as it was with many appetizing dishes cooked in German style. At night I had a genuine feather bed, the kind in which you lose yourself, and for cover a soft feather comforter of ample proportions light as down. I marched my wagon train back to Fort Wadsworth in good order, turned over the supplies to the quartermaster, and resumed my duties with the company.

Early in the spring of 1867 the company was ordered to establish a station at the forks of the Cheyenne River near Bear's Den Hill toward the northern boundary of Dakota Territory. The Cheyenne enters the Red River near the site of old Fort Assiniboin.

Our course led over a rolling prairie. Nothing of interest occurred until the second or third day, when we crossed a high and level plain which extended for many miles. This plain was covered with a thin coating of ice, and on all sides as far as the eye could reach was dotted with the bodies of dead buffaloes. These animals were in good condition and bore no mark of bullet or arrow wounds. The cause of their death was a mystery to us. As we marched over the plain toward the valley of the

Cheyenne the appearance of so many carcasses scattered around made a strong impression on my mind, perhaps because they were the first buffaloes I had ever seen.

Bear's Den Hill proved to be merely a grass-covered knob with no romantic associations attached to it as far as I could learn. The adjacent country was a rolling plain, bare of timber except along streams and in the coulees, and it contained but little game. Judged by the standards of the present day our situation was cheerless enough. We constructed rude quarters of logs, floored with boards and lighted by candles. Our daily ration consisted of salt pork, bacon, beans, rice, dried apples, and peaches, together with coffee and tea. Milk we procured only at rare intervals. We always had sweet fresh bread, however, and were supplied with beef by contract. Notwithstanding our rude quarters and simple fare, we were as happy and cheerful as soldiers could be.

For the evening meal we marched through a dark corridor, cold as ice, to the kitchen, where the cook and his assistant dished out a pint of tea and a good-sized chunk of bread, while as a side dish there was usually a plate of cold boiled pork from which each soldier might help himself. Having procured our share of pork, we returned with it to our quarters, where we ate our meal. I do not remember that any officer ever inspected or witnessed the issue of food except at Sunday morning inspection.

Some time in the winter of 1867-1868 Colonel Whistler came down from the post at Devil's Lake to inspect our command. He was a handsome man with black curly hair. I did not see him again until 1876, when he was serving as second in command to General Miles at a cantonment on Tongue River, Montana. Here I witnessed an affray between some Cheyenne warriors and the Crows which will be described in a subsequent chapter.

My term of enlistment was drawing to its close and at last the day came when I was to bid good-by to soldier life. I was too much enamored with the free full life of prairie and mountain to suffer the restriction and discipline of another period of service in the army, especially in time of peace. There is nothing finer for a young fellow than a three-year term in the United States army, for it teaches him method, manliness, physical welfare, and obedience to authority. One enlistment is sufficient, however, unless one wishes to make soldiering a profession.

CHAPTER II

FROM FORT RANSOM TO THE YELLOWSTONE

I T was early spring when I left Fort Ransom. The only conveyance to the outside world was by dog sled, which also carried the United States mail. This meant that my bundle would find place on the sled while I followed in the footsteps of the driver, whose muscles had been hardened by months of such travel. I managed to keep up with him during the first thirty or forty miles, though not without making some strong drafts on my store of reserve energy. After that my recollection is not clear as to how I reached the end of the first stage of travel at Fort Abercrombie. Here I took the regular stage for St. Paul, the place where my pay vouchers were to be cashed. I remember passing Ottertail Lake, and I have no doubt the route led through a beautiful country, but when we traversed it, early in April, it was flooded with the melting snows and we seemed to be traveling for miles through shallow lakes.

When my business at St. Paul was completed I embarked upon a project I had long cherished. This was to proceed to the Canadian settlement of Fort Garry and from there journey westward, wherever the spirit of adventure might lead me, until I had reached the wild country at the headwaters of the Missouri River.

One day in May, 1868, when I had left the scattered farms behind me, I found myself following a wagon track that led north down the Red River Valley, through a land of gentle slopes. The rich soil nourished succulent grasses and legumes; all the cattle in the state of Minnesota could have grazed in this valley for a month without injuring its value as a pasture land. But there were no cattle and I encountered no buffaloes; only a few deer now and then broke the monotony of the landscape.

At night I halted near running water where wood was handy, and picketing my pony in some good grass, proceeded to make camp. I first built a fire and when this was going well I cut an armful of coarse dry grass for my bed. Then I loosened the small bundle that was tied behind my saddle and took from it a quart tin for boiling coffee, a small frying pan, and the tin that fitted into it, a cup, and a small sack of flour. Then I went to the stream for water.

By this time the fire had become a mass of coals. I mixed up a lump of dough in the pan, added baking-powder and salt to it, and then I raked out a lot of coals on which I placed the frying pan at an angle, propping it with a stick so that the heat would strike the bread from both sides. When the bread had swelled out like a baked potato I removed it and stood it up to keep hot while I used the skillet to cook the bacon or fresh meat.

Bread baked in this way is sweet and satisfying. If you do not happen to have a frying pan the dough may be twisted around a green stick and baked by sticking the end in the ground near the fire. The entire act is accomplished before coffee is made. Of course the camper's outfit is not complete without a Dutch oven, but there is no sweeter hot bread than that made before the open fire.

One night I stopped with a Frenchman who seemed to be a man of culture, but as he could not speak English

16

and I could not talk French we could not exchange ideas. At length I crossed a river on a flatboat ferry and mounting my pony rode through a scattered settlement until I came to a modest hostelry, where I put up. I had reached Fort Garry, as it was then known, where now is the thriving city of Winnipeg.

Among the boarders at the hotel were a number of Montana miners who had "come across" to winter on Red River, as the living was much cheaper here than it was in the mining towns of Montana. They were very friendly toward the "tenderfoot traveler," and I found much pleasure in their company. They told me a great deal, too, about the country through which they had traveled in coming from the Missouri River. When I said that I was going that way they shook their heads and sought to dissuade me. "When you get near the Missouri," they said, "you are bound to run into war parties. The Sioux are continually at war with the Ree, Grosventres, and Mandan and it would be duck soup for them to meet a lone white man." Such talk as this was discouraging, nevertheless I was determined to go ahead, trusting to fall in with some of the people going out to make pemmican.

On my journey to Fort Garry I had met no Indians except on one occasion. On the road through Minnesota I was halted one day at a small river running through a swamp. The crossing looked difficult and while I was deliberating how best to accomplish it I saw close at hand a large birch-bark canoe filled with Indians in bright costume, stealing silently along. It was a beautiful sight, though startling at first. The gaily decorated canoe, the handsome young men that manned it, their garments garnished with bead, feather, and porcupine-quill work, the slow easy movement of the paddles, all in a setting of green forest that bordered the sluggish stream, formed a picture that has fixed itself in my memory.

The warriors turned in slowly to my side where I sat on a tree trunk. They stayed silently with paddle, and one, evidently a leader, spoke and gestured at the same time, saying as plainly as though it had been uttered in English, "What is your trouble?" I have since seen the same sign among the prairie Indians; it is called the hailing sign, and means: "Who are you; what is the matter?" or "What do you want?"

I recognized the language of my visitors as the Chippewa. They understood English but did not speak it. They were very friendly. They not only took me across the river in their canoe, while I led the pony at the end of the lariat, but they gave me at parting three roasted muskrats, on which I made an excellent meal.

The Montana miners put the pack on my pony and lashed it on with the "diamond hitch," which was new to me, and I tried to make the same knot when next I loaded the pony, but failed on the combination. The man who later taught me how to pack claimed that he could put thirteen empty flour barrels on a pack mule saddled with an *aparejo* [pack saddle], and lash them on with the diamond hitch. Whatever skill I obtained as a packer is due to the instruction of Christopher Gilson, an old-timer well known to many old army officers who, if still living, are now on the retired list.

At length all was ready and I started, westward bound for the Missouri River. Although I had seen three years of soldier life I was not yet nineteen. On foot and leading my pony I passed through several settlements of half-breeds; in one the French predominated, in another the English, and in a third the Scotch. The French settlement was the largest of the three. In one village I found a Yankee storekeeper by the name of House.

One day a native stopped me on the road and said: "Why travel afoot and make your horse's back sore with light saddle? I will sell you one wooden cart and you ride and carry load." His offer was specious enough, but I was not in the market that day for a Red River cart, so I shook my head and answered, "No, thank you."

At the crossing of the Assiniboin River I fell in with a party of English half-breeds with their carts, bound for the buffalo grounds to make pemmican. They invited me to join their party, which I gladly did, and shifting my pack to one of the carts I mounted my steed and rode with the horsemen at the head of the train.

One of the first things to strike my fancy was a blue broadcloth Red River coat with hood attached, and I lost no time in purchasing one. This style of garment is of an ancient pattern and probably dates from the early days when the Hudson's Bay Company supplied an enormous trade in clothing to strike the fancy of a host of employees, voyageurs, and fur traders. The cloth furnished by this company was of the very best quality and their blankets, in particular, were much esteemed and in great demand in the western country in those days. The coats were made of a good grade of blue broadcloth and ornamented with flat brass buttons. The blankets were of all colors, but the trade was mostly in red and black, which seemed to meet the fancy of the

traders and Indians above other colors. They were of
different grades and were marked with small black bars
in one corner; thus, a four-point blanket was heavy and
commanded the highest price. American goods were of
such shoddy material as not to compare with English
goods in the Far West.

With my blue coat and red sash I felt more like a
free lance of the prairie, especially while with these half-
breed buffalo hunters, who made the prairie their home
a good part of the year. There were about twelve or
fourteen families in the party. Some had pitched skin
lodges similar to the Sioux tepee, others used canvas in
place of skins for covering the conical framework of
poles, while a few families had canvas tents. I slept on
the ground under a cart in the open air.

The carts were made wholly of wood, and not a single
nail or bolt entered into their construction. The rims of
the high wheels were covered with strips of raw bull's
hide laced on while green, making very effective tires,
hard and durable as iron, and so light that the carts
would float while the ponies swam across streams.

We saw no game but antelopes on the rolling plains
until after we had passed Mouse River. At this stream
we feasted on fish which the half-breeds called "gold-
eyes." Their method of cooking them, however, did not
appeal to me, as the custom was to boil them in a pot,
heads and all. At night, after everyone else had retired,
a young man of the party brought a good-sized fish and
baked it on a slab in front of the fire. I thought it most
delicious.

It was on Mouse River that I first came in contact
with Sitting Bull and his war party. As we were going
into camp one day a party of horsemen suddenly came

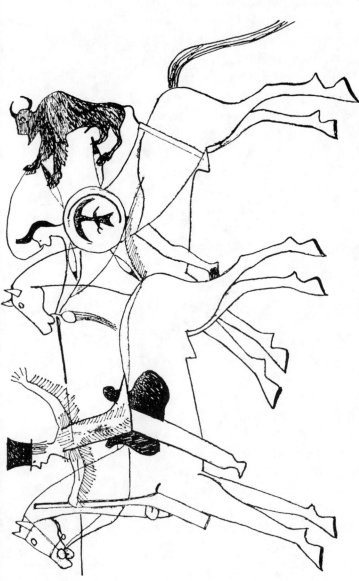

SITTING BULL

Whose sign is shown in the picture, shoots and scalps a frontiersman, hangs the scalp
on his bridle, and captures the horse.

Pictograph (1868), copied from an Indian Buffalo Robe.

into view, and approaching rapidly, dismounted and went through our party shaking hands right and left, using both hands in the process, which struck me as singular in an Indian.

In our party were a man and a woman of the Santee Sioux. Of course they told Sitting Bull that I was an American and the warriors gathered around me where I stood with my rifle in hand. The old man with whom I messed had assured me that though we might meet hostile Indians I would come to no harm as long as I stayed with the party, so I looked them calmly in the eye while they thronged about me, regarding me with baleful eyes, hate and vindictiveness pervading every feature of their villainous faces. Without a word they abruptly left me, and mounting their horses, soon passed out of sight.

Sitting Bull appeared to be about thirty years of age. He had a round, pleasant face, and wore a headscarf of dirty white cloth, while most of his followers affected black headgear. I suspected that the stiff leather cases tied to some of the saddles contained war bonnets, as I saw feathers sticking out of the pouches. They assume their war regalia when on the war path, though they usually strip to the breechclout when going into action. They were armed with rifles and trade shotguns in addition to the usual bow and quiver of arrows. They reported killing a white man a short time before near the mouth of the Yellowstone.

That night I kept my rifle very close to where I slept. In the night there came a sprinkle of rain and the old half-breed came out of his lodge to adjust the cover on the cart and accidentally trod near my head. Like a flash I was on my feet with gun cocked and pointing at his head. He was speechless with fright and I with consternation, realizing how near I had come to shooting him, which would have been a great calamity in my situation.

In trembling accents he said: "Would you shoot me, boy?"

"I was sound asleep," I replied, "and thought it was the war party stealing into camp."

These people did not make pemmican while I was with them, as I left before the meat was dry enough to work up, but having witnessed the process many times since then I will describe it here for the reader.

The buffaloes being killed, and scattered over a considerable area of ground, all hands turn in and cut up the meat, which is packed to camp. Here it is cut into great slabs the thickness of one's finger and hung on long lines of rawhide or lariat to dry in the sun. When thoroughly dry the meat, much reduced in weight and size, is toasted slightly on coals, then placed on rawhides or stiff canvas and broken up as much as possible with flails very much like those used for threshing wheat.

The desiccated meat is then placed in rawhide sacks and the mass is solidified by pouring in hot tallow or marrow fat, and the sacks are fastened with rawhide thongs in much the same way that sacks of grain are tied. One pound of this wholesome and concentrated food is equal to about ten pounds of fresh meat. It will keep in good condition one or two years, and the Red River people sold tons of it to the trade posts on both sides of the line, besides conserving great quantities for their own winter use and for sale in the settlements. The desiccated meat, fresh from contact with live coals, is most appetizing and sustaining, and when mixed with marrow fat it makes a rich food. A pony will pull from 1000 to 1500 pounds on a cart, and the pemmican is usually made at a time of the year when the fur on the buffalo is not in condition for a robe.

We were now on the prairie away from timber, somewhere north of Devil's Lake, and as we neared the divide that sloped to the Missouri River I looked forward to leaving these simple, friendly people, who prayed on Sunday, chased buffaloes regardless of prairie-dog holes, and drank tea without sweetening. At last the morning came when the old half-breed said: "We will make the adventure this day." We rode a few miles to some rising ground which he called the "Coteau des Prairies" and there we parted. "Look out for the Sioux, boy," was his parting injunction, as he pointed in the direction I was to follow.

I rode leisurely along until I had topped the low divide of grassland, with here and there scrub timber in the hollows and ravines, and from this viewpoint I saw, not the valley of the Missouri, but the country beyond, with rough hills and ridges covered with dark timber like cedar. It seemed a forbidding-looking country, under the shadow of low-lying clouds far on the western horizon. It was, indeed, a land of broils and feuds, where dwelt many tribes of men of different tongues, whose pastime was war until the white man came, who warred against none, but fought all, because opposed.

I rode at a good pace and suddenly arrived on the bank of the great Missouri, which rolled along between narrow bluffs with no valley or timber on either side. Perhaps not in hundreds of miles could the river have presented to the stranger a more unattractive aspect than at the bend where I touched it. Yet its potential power, mighty in its confinement between gray bluffs of sandstone, was apparent at once.

Man and horse took a refreshing drink of mighty *Minnishushu,* then I marked the places where Lewis and Clark's boatmen must have trod while cordelling their clumsy boats up the river, for there was no shifting of the channel in that rockbound bend.

Ascending the nearest hill below this point, I descried two horsemen on a similar point about a mile farther down the valley. I rode slowly in their direction and when I had reached low ground out of their sight I changed my course so that when next I sighted them I was several hundred yards to the left of the direct approach. They had not moved, and reassured, I made directly for them.

I found them to be two young men who were guarding bands of ponies that I now saw scattered along the rolling plains beyond. I could readily see that these men were not Sioux, but had different features and dress. Instead of wearing their hair in two rolls wrapped in fur, the two coils hanging in front were garnished with white discs of shell or mother-of-pearl, while the forehead was embellished with an upright brush of hair stiffened with white clay. I had picked up a few signs, so I asked them where the camp was; they pointed down the river and indicated by the sun that it was about one hour's ride. "Any white people?" I inquired. They said that there were plenty of whites and asked where I came from, and by the way they eyed my costume I surmised that they took me for a Red River man, and classed me as friendly to their enemies, the Sioux.

I passed on presently and noted that the country ahead widened out into a valley several miles in extent and was heavily wooded along the river bends. Finally, I saw a collection of buildings and a flagpole on a low bluff just above the river. A nearer approach disclosed a village of round, earth-covered huts, with here and there one or more Indians perched on top, like prairie dogs on their mounds.

I was an object of curiosity as I rode by, but I did not stop until I had reached the center, or front, of the more pretentious buildings I had first sighted.

I soon found that I had arrived at Fort Berthold, an Indian agency for the Arikara, Grosventres, and Mandan, who lived amicably together for mutual protection against their hereditary enemies, the Sioux.

The United States agent, a most amiable man, whose name I cannot now recall, kindly allowed me to eat at the agency mess, and later placed me on the agency rolls until I had in a manner found myself.

Being of an inquisitive disposition in those days, I lost no time in looking about, for the place was replete with new and interesting associations. Out on the plain a short distance was an extensive Indian burial ground, where the dead were elevated on platforms supported on slender poles, on which were suspended the arms and equipment of the departed, while underneath on the ground were strewn all sorts of paraphernalia that an Indian would require on his entrance to the happy hunting grounds, all in various stages of disintegration and decay. Years before, the smallpox had descended upon the village and taken heavy toll. The disease was aggravated by the native custom of taking sweat baths and immediately jumping into the river.

Close by the agency but nearer the river bank stood the trading establishment. This was a stockade affair with a strong gate that was closed and locked at night. Inside were the country store and a dwelling or two. The representative, like the Indian agent, was a very decent gentleman, but reticent, not given much to conversation. Behind the counters was displayed a line of goods calculated to touch the heart or desires of the red man—bolts of coarse broadcloth, red and blue ornamental shells and beads, knives and hatchets, shawls and headbands, powder in kegs and brown sugar in barrels, flints and matches, trade guns and a variety of blankets, and many other goods to catch the eye.

The trader had a few Henry carbines, but they were for the white trade. Before I left Fort Berthold I purchased one of these carbines and it served me well for several years, or until I was able to secure a Winchester rifle. With the Henry and the stubby little .44 caliber cartridge that went with it I killed many a buffalo, as well as other game, and it stood me in good hand when I was forced to defend myself in encounters with hostile Indians.

There was also another store in a different part of the post kept by the Gerard brothers, who were free lances in the Indian trade, the older of whom was an old timer in the Indian country. He was later with Reno in Custer's last fight and ran a narrow escape from being captured when Reno turned back.

In the sixties and early seventies there was much fighting in the region about Fort Berthold. The vast country across the river was a stronghold of the Sioux, who greatly outnumbered the agency Indians. The latter could go to the distant hunting grounds only in strong parties. I saw them bring their ponies up at night in great bands and take them out again in the morning. They had fields of Indian corn and squashes in the bottom land and on these and the dried meat from their caches of the winter's hunt they lived sumptuously through the summer and harvest while they dried the sweet corn and squashes for winter use. On my way to the Indian encampment I stopped at the log store of the Gerard brothers. This store contained a smaller but perhaps better selected class of goods for the Indian trade than the larger establishment. There was keen competition all along the river.

The Indians usually came in groups to trade, but a single family would sometimes ask for a private deal and the shop would be closed to the others while it was being carried on.

While I was there an Indian came in with a very fine buffalo cow robe with some pictograph writing in pigment colors of some Indian scene or event faintly outlined on the fleshy side. I noticed that the half-breed who waited on him in measuring out twenty-five pint cups of brown sugar to pay for the robe kept his thumb full length in the cup, thereby subtracting from full measure in each portion, which I found to be a common practice.

It was told, though I cannot vouch for it, that the Gerards made their initial stake by being first on the scene after a party of Montana miners descending the river in a small boat with considerable gold dust on board had been attacked and killed by hostile Indians, who shook the sacks of gold dust into the boat, having no use for such stuff or being ignorant of its value.

I now proceeded to the village, which began only a few yards beyond the trade store. Imagine a good-sized village of round, earth-covered houses, each with a small opening at the top to serve for ventilation and as an outlet for the smoke of the fires built directly underneath. In constructing these houses a stout square framework of wood was first erected and around this slabs were placed in circular form and above wooden rafters in rounding form, the whole being plastered with mud and covered with grass, on which earth was heaped to make a covering a foot or more thick.

These houses were warm in winter and delightfully cool in summer. From the housetops warriors harangued the settlement or recounted the latest news. Here the members of the family gathered after the heat of the day to gossip with their neighbors or for observation when anything novel or exciting took place. Across the river lay a broad sand bar, with a forest of timber stretching to the low-lying hills beyond. In their light bull boats the natives crossed the river for wood, and when an enemy suddenly appeared the river was alive with boats loaded with warriors, with their ponies swimming behind. A boat made of one bull-hide held four or more men and their arms; no saddles were used on the occasion of an alarm, only the lariat tied around the pony's jaw to guide him.

In fair weather the entrance to the dwellings was left open. I entered one and found a spacious interior fairly lighted from the aperture above, and the air odorous of the fragrant shrubwood used as fuel on the open fire in the center. Along the sides, robes and blankets were disposed to form couches and sleeping places. I was greeted with "How! how!" and given the place of honor farthest from the door.

Without a word an old fellow filled a long-stemmed pipe with a mixture of tobacco and red willow bark, which the Dakotas call *chashasha,* reached for a coal, and lighting it, puffed thoughtfully for a moment and then passed the pipe to me. I took it, for I was familiar with the Indian custom, and though not at that time a user of tobacco in any form, essayed a few whiffs and returned it in the same manner.

Some abodes in this village were ornamented with reed screens and bright-colored cottons, and many were roomy enough to stable two or more ponies in time of strife or cold at one side of the living space. When the room was filled with young men and women and their voices rose in unison to the chant of love or festival songs there was some noise from the rude orchestra, but a world of melody and feeling wild and sweet, differing from the low wild chant of male voices that I once listened to from my concealment in a wood within fifty feet of a war party encamped on a dark night just on the edge of a forest on the upper river.

The harvest festival and ceremonial attending the initiation of the young Indian into the duties of a warrior is the greatest event of the year among these allied people. It has been too often described for me to undertake the task here, but I cannot refrain from observing that the spectacle of a young man suspended by thongs thrust through slits cut through the skin of his back, there to hang until flesh and skin give way under the exertions of the ardent and longing victim, which proclaims him as one unafraid and able to endure, would afford a thrilling picture for some moving picture promoter of the present day.

When engaged in the chase or in strife the warriors of the Fort Berthold agency led a most active life, but at other times their life was one of ease and relaxation.

After their sweat baths, to which they were much addicted, I have seen them stalk down to the river bank in groups or singly, wrapped in robes like a Roman toga, for the daily plunge. When they returned from the bath, face, body, and hair were plastered with strips of white clay.

The sweat bath was a simple affair. A circular framework was made by sticking willows into the ground so as to make a round top. Over this pieces of canvas, robes, or skins were hung to make the wickiup as airtight as possible. Then a fire was built over and around a pile of rocks until they were well heated. With a green willow looped, these are transferred to the interior of the wickiup and the bathers being seated naked around the center, a little water is dropped on the red-hot rocks, producing a cloud of steam which at first almost suffocates the bather. At once a feeling of joyful languor diffuses itself through the body and expels pain and fatigue. Ten minutes is enough, and the after-plunge into cold water is only for the strong and vigorous, cooling water and a rub being sufficient to close the pores in any temperature.

There is nothing just like the vapor bath in an Indian sweat house in its good effects; you recline on a robe on the ground while the water oozes from every pore. An Indian may have traveled fifty or a hundred miles in the saddle or afoot, or danced all day and all night; he will then immediately hie himself to a sweat bath and feel invigorated for new efforts.

I suspect that in the sixties an Indian agent was very much a free lance, untroubled by inspectors, with reservation boundaries rather vaguely defined. Here all was Indian country. From the Missouri River westward to the mountains stretched a vast terrain peopled only by Indians. The land swarmed with game, so that one could ride north for hundreds of miles and never be out of sight of buffaloes and their attendant friends, the agile, keen-eyed antelopes, who gave the alarm on approach of danger.

I wish I could remember the name of the agent who honored his office in the year 1868 at Fort Berthold. The Indians respected him, and I believe him to have been a faithful servant of the government. Of the white men living at the fort I remember George Milford, tall, quiet, and reserved; also Mike Welsh, a great hunter and trapper.

Among the Indian chiefs there were some very fine men. I can recall by name one, Sun of the Star, in whose lodge I was always welcome. Years later, I was to meet him again after the Nez Percé campaign. I had come across country from the Yellowstone with General Miles and others who were in an ambulance, and at a turn of the road about ten miles from Fort Berthold I saw, a little way off, a group of Indians standing on either side of the road. I was riding in advance and pushed on to see who they were, while the ambulance stopped. They proved to be from Fort Berthold and the chief Sun of the Star, recognizing me, shook my hand heartily, as did the rest. The General then came up and the chiefs greeted him. After a few words of pow-wow, mostly in the sign language, all started on and at Berthold, where we remained for the night, there was a council with the chiefs.

When November came I grew restless. I had heard so many stories of the upper river and its doings that I longed for a change of scene. One day I went over to the palisaded store and purchased one of the brass-mounted little Henry carbines that I have spoken of, along with a supply of .44 caliber cartridges. If I remember correctly I paid fifty dollars for the outfit.

Next morning, with two woolen blankets strapped on my back and a belt of ammunition with knife and case around me, I started on foot up the river into the unknown. I kept along the river bank, as the ice which covered it in some places made it easy to cut the bends and there was less likelihood of meeting unfriendly people on the way.

I saw no game that day, as I was too close to the agency for hunting. Late in the afternoon I tried my new gun on a couple of prairie chickens that were foolish enough to leave the seclusion of the thick brush and linger in the branches of a cottonwood tree. I aimed for the neck, as there are two chances against one for missing. Then I went on a little way and built a fire in the brush, and spitting one of the chickens on a green willow, held it against the fire until it was done brown. Hunger being in a manner appeased, I rested awhile before proceeding until it was so dark that I could not see my way. I then made camp in the willows without a fire, which I disliked, as the night was cold. I had but a double blanket and there was no dry grass or willows to gather to temper the hardness of the frozen ground.

At the first streak of dawn I was up and had scarcely started on my way when I disturbed two deer that broke through the brush and were gone. I continued on and had gone but a few hundred yards when I suddenly came upon a small Indian encampment of log huts in a little clearing. It proved to be one of the winter camps of the Fort Berthold Indians, a family group of Mandan. Although it was scarcely daylight these people were already stirring about. I opened a door where I saw a light through the chinks of the cabin, and they bade me enter. The light came from a fireplace in a chimney plastered with clay, and it served the purpose well, being about twenty inches deep and four or five feet in width. It was built with a slope like the rake of a mast on a yacht, and the fuel was stood on end, so that a generous light and heat pervaded the room as long as it lasted.

In this room were several Indian men and women, but the hostess appeared to be one Mag Pease, a woman celebrated in her day, tall, stately, intelligent, well-bred, and hospitable, and held in high esteem by all who knew her. There was also Sally Four-Bears, daughter of a well-known chief. They gave me some parched corn and dried meat for breakfast and urged me to stay with them until the next day. I was glad to do so, and I spent half a day to no purpose trying to pick up the tracks of the deer I had encountered in the willows.

In the evening a few sticks of cottonwood thrown on the fireplace made a bright light, and seated in a circle on robes disposed on the floor the people questioned me as to where I came from and why I had left such pleasant scenes to live in a wild country where there were only wild creatures and a few white men.

I answered by asking if some of their young men did not sometimes travel to distant countries and visit other tribes who spoke a strange language, and come back after months or years of absence to relate their adventures. I was like them, I said. I liked to travel amid ever changing scenes. Meanwhile, the pipe circulated among the men and a pot was placed on the fire with meat and dried squash and corn, and we ate and talked far into the night, a young woman who spoke good English acting as our interpreter.

At last the fire died down and the robes were spread for those who slept in the house. My blankets were spread near the center of the room and I was asked if I wanted a young woman to sleep with. I laughed and replied no, that I invariably slept alone while in this country, and in the best language I could command said that it was against my medicine to change my mind in the matter. With this they were satisfied, and I believe that the offer was made in courtesy and with no thought of immorality and impropriety.

Presently, observing that most of the women had retired to their several sleeping places, I removed my moccasins and with my coat for a pillow reclined on the robe assigned me, covering myself with my blanket. An aged Indian stood a few chips of dry cottonwood on end in the fireplace, where they quickly blazed into a roaring flame and almost as quickly fell amid a shower of sparks. I fell asleep and woke only when a swarm of Indian dogs in the early morning gave voice to a weird chorus in emulation of a pack of wolves which was serenading the camp from the near-by hills.

After I had breakfasted on toasted dried meat and corn I bade adieu to my hosts and resumed my journey, and soon found a fair trail leading to the next winter encampment. Late in the day I reached it, and entering one of the log huts was greeted with loud cries of "How! how!" by a group of warriors who until my entrance on the scene had been absorbed in watching a big pot of meat and dried corn boiling in the fireplace. The master of ceremonies was an old Indian who was armed with a slender wooden paddle, with which he occasionally stirred the mess, licking the paddle off with his tongue. I was invited to join the circle, and finding that they lacked *minnesquea,* as salt is called by the Sioux, I produced a handful from my supplies and it was added to the broth.

I also became absorbed in watching the finishing touches of that pot of Indian "mulligan." The old fellow now changed his method of manipulating the paddle, for on removing it after a vigorous stir, he used his forefinger in transferring the oily drippings to his mouth. Apparently the dish was now cooked, for he signed to another Indian to remove the pot from the fire, and, dishes of wood, stone, and copper being brought, a general distribution was made in which each one received a share, there being none left after the last man was served. I ate my portion until the first sting of hunger was appeased without calling to mind the incident of the paddle and the Indian who was so partial to it. Indeed, I have taken food in an Indian camp where I suspected that dog was served, and found that dog was not so bad after all. The usual pipe followed and made the rounds of the circle, then a young boy piloted me to another cabin, where I was regaled with bruised dried buffalo meat and a chunk of pure white marrow fat that was sweet and good. Not being served with knife and fork I used my fingers in breaking the meat and cut bits of the marrow with my knife in the trencher containing the food. A pipe followed, of which I was fain to take a whiff or two, then came a call from outside the door and my host signed for me to go. I was led to another cabin and on entering found the people ready for me with a fine robe folded near the fireplace for a seat and a soft piece of parfleche in front of it as a spread. Seating myself in response to a gesture, an old squaw brought a cast-iron tea kettle and served me an excellent dish of coffee and with it a dish of cold boiled venison.

Truly these people intended to fill me with good things, and though I had already had enough I was fain to stow away what was before me for fear of offending my entertainers, one of whom I recognized as a man I had befriended once upon a time at Fort Berthold, when the trader refused to let him have some tobacco on credit. "Bring your things," he said, "and sleep on that robe tonight."

When I was ready to turn in, four or five young women entered and made merry at my expense, asking if I always traveled alone and if I did not get lonesome, and if I was not afraid of meeting a war party of the Sioux, to all of which they received little satisfaction because of my inability to converse in the Mandan tongue. Suddenly one of the young women asked if I would give her one of my red blankets. I was in a quandary, for I needed both of my red blankets badly on the road. Picking one up, however, I folded it neatly and held it out with both arms, but before she could take it the people of the house scolded the young women out of the room and they went away, laughing and unconcerned.

In the morning, after I had eaten and was preparing to start on my way, my host said: "My son will accompany you and show you the road as far as the Painted Woods. From there on there is a road traveled by wagons."

"Good," I replied, "and if the sign is good we may

camp and look for deer and elk." The young man was about my own age and carried a very indifferent-looking shotgun.

The trail ran very straight across the sand bars and bends where the banks were favorable, but it was not used by horsemen on account of the ice being bare of snow. We were ten miles on our way before any fresh deer sign appeared; we then crossed trail after trail of bands heading for the cedar ridges on the south side.

Proceeding with more caution now, we presently came upon a band of about fifty strung out along an opening in the cottonwoods and I shot two without difficulty. The next task was to dress them and then hang them up on a tree out of reach of the wolves. In this work the Indian was much more at home than I, and he handled the buck in half the time that I was occupied with the doe. They were black-tails, and though poor in flesh were heavy animals.

The timber was all large, but I found a leaning cottonwood tree with low limbs, on which with some labor and the use of a short elk-skin lariat that the Indian had we elevated the two deer out of reach of prowling animals. The Mandan said that some of his people would find the meat on the following day and that he would return to camp with them. He tore a strip from his turban and attached it to a limb of the tree for the information of those who should follow us.

Reaching the Painted Woods late in the day, we found numerous signs of game. We camped near the cedar ridges in the river bottom, where I shot a young buck. Selecting a spot where the thick brush would absorb the light of our fire and cutting a lot of coarse dry grass for beds, we proceeded to roast ribs and brisket until our hunger was satisfied. Another dish was prepared by the Mandan that tasted very good. Taking the larger intestine of the deer, he rubbed it clean in the snow and then engaging it on the ramrod of his gun turned it inside out. Having tied one end with a bit of sinew, the container was ready for business. This was accomplished by cutting bits of lean meat, adding some buffalo marrow fat that he extracted from a parfleche sack in his belongings, and stuffing the whole into the intestine until he had produced a rough-looking sausage, when he tied the other end and laid it gently on a fine bed of coals which I had raked out for the purpose. Here it was slowly cooked, exuding, meanwhile, a rich aroma which gave promise of a feast not to be despised.

Before daylight my companion had built a fire and set to work roasting some more ribs for our breakfast. This was our parting place. I was to kill a couple of deer which he would take back to his father if he should succeed in intercepting some of his people, as he expected to do.

I was in no hurry, for the distance to Fort Buford at the mouth of the Yellowstone was not great and I was loath to part with the Indian as he had shown manly qualities, and while I could not understand much of what he said, he was cheerful and helpful at all times.

It was evening when I came in sight of the collection of buildings that constituted the "fort." In reality it was more of a cantonment, as it had no stockade around it, as I remember. Situated in the bend of the Missouri as it sweeps down from the junction, it was bounded on the north by a rolling prairie which extended for a couple of miles to the foothills and afforded a grazing ground for buffaloes as late as the early seventies. A couple of miles higher up the river stood the ruins of old Fort Union, which had been a famous trading post in its day.

CHAPTER III

CARRYING THE MAIL TO FORT STEVENSON

I HAD been at Fort Buford but a little while when I learned that an important mail was about to leave for the lower post at Fort Stevenson. The military mail at that time was carried by two civilians, friends of mine, George Parshall and a man called Dutch, who took their lives in their hands about twice a month. These riders were now long overdue and it was thought that they had met misfortune at the hands of hostile Indians. Special inducements (with no takers) were being offered by the authorities to anyone who would volunteer in their place. I was in need of employment, and concluded to apply for the vacant job. When I presented myself to the officer in charge and offered to convey the mail to Fort Stevenson alone, a shout of laughter went up from a group of men standing near by, who had overheard the conversation. I insisted that I was in earnest, however, and the officer finally consented to give me a trial. I decided to start at dusk, since this would enable me to pass through some of the most dangerous portion of the road in the darkness.

Late in the afternoon, with a little packet of mail secured under my belt I wended my way to the quartermaster's stable for my mount. The stable was a long, rambling structure built of logs, cool in summer and warm in winter, and I felt the genial heat as soon as I entered. There were two or three soldiers in attendance, who soon brought forth my steed ready saddled and bridled. They held him by the head while I adjusted one of my three-point blankets under the packet of grain that was strapped to the pig-skin army saddle. I then had leisure to survey my mount. And such a mount! He was a mustang of the prairie, a roan with a chocolate-colored stripe down his backbone.

The man held him by the bit as I took the reins and vaulted lightly into the saddle. He did not require any pressure to start, but shot out of the stable in a way that made me suspect he had not been exercised of late. I let him have his head until he became used to the frosty air; having in mind the long hard journey, I then tried to check him, but he did not respond to my endeavor and kept his gait untrammeled until we had gone a considerable distance. We then proceeded at a more moderate pace over the snow-covered, icy trail. I was now headed for the Mandan camp where I had stopped on my journey from Fort Berthold earlier in the winter.

It was after midnight when I rode into the clearing where the cabins stood, but in one or two of them the lights were still shining. A young Indian came out of a large cabin and invited me to enter. As I dismounted the bronco seemed to have discovered for the first time that I wore a shirt of buffalo calfskin with the hair left on. He snorted and struck at me with his fore foot and despite my efforts to hold him broke loose and disappeared into the misty night. I let him go and entered the lodge with the young man. It proved to be a tepee set up against a log hut that had a fireplace, before which several young men were feasting on buffalo ribs. It appeared to be some sort of young men's club or social organization.

I placed my gun and trappings to one side and sat

down on a buffalo robe near the genial heat of the fire. Presently a wooden bowl of meat broth was brought and placed on a piece of stiff parfleche, to which a couple of broiled buffalo ribs were soon added, and I lost no time in making a very satisfactory repast.

As yet no one had spoken a word to me, but now, hunger satisfied, a long pipe was produced and by a simple gesture of the sign language I was asked to contribute the "makings." I reached for the plug of tobacco that I carried for such emergencies, and cutting it in two gave one-half to the pipe-holder, who shaved off the necessary amount to mix with a proper quantity of Indian tobacco. This is of two kinds; the bark of the red willow or "kinnikinic," and a low creeping plant with glossy, dark green leaves, found only in certain situations near the mountains and commonly known as "larb." Either kind, when mixed with an equal amount of the tobacco of commerce, affords a mild and fragrant smoke.

Conversation now unfolded and I was asked for the news from up river. As best I could in broken Sioux I gave them what news I had, and they told of an exciting hunt to the head breaks of the little Missouri, where they had killed so many elk and mountain sheep that they had been compelled to pack all of their horses, and themselves foot it to their village on the Missouri. They also lamented the scarcity of buffaloes, which by constant hunting had been driven off their usual range toward the country of the Sioux.

Presently a young man came to the door of the lodge and beckoned me. I went out and found that they had driven my steed into a lariat corral. I caught him, and removing the saddle and bridle, tied him to a tree, where he soon devoured the feed that the stablemen at Fort

Carrying the Mail

Buford had been thoughtful enough to provide. A young Indian now brought him some sticks of green cottonwood, but the animal did not savvy that kind of food and would not touch it. I noticed in the morning, however, that the bark had been peeled clean from the wood.

I slept sweetly on a robe in the lodge until daylight routed me out. With some difficulty I saddled the irrepressible mustang and proceeded on my way. I encountered only friendly Indians along the trail, which ran through cottonwood much of the way, with frequent crossings of the river, and without further incident reached the stockaded camp of Red Mike, where I received a joyful welcome from that lonely trapper.

Mike was a fearless hunter, who had many narrow escapes from the Sioux. He related one amusing adventure with a friendly Arikara. While hunting one day he saw what he took for a jack rabbit in the edge of the timber. This was very small game but it would make a stew for his dinner. He could see the ears flapping back, and taking a hasty aim he fired. Much to his surprise, up jumped an Indian who had been mending his moccasins. He had a white rag tied round his head with the ends sticking up, and as he sewed away the swaying head looked very much like a rabbit. The Indian was scared as well as furious, and as Mike approached, he exclaimed, "You tried to kill me." Mike protested that he had mistaken him for a rabbit. "You fool!" said the Indian scornfully, "Who ever saw a jack rabbit in the woods!" Mike never got through paying this Indian; every time they met there was a demand for tobacco, sugar, powder, or some other commodity.

Next day I reached Fort Berthold, and then pushed

on for Fort Stevenson. Of the ride down from Fort Berthold I now remember nothing, but I have a distinct recollection of inquiring for the commander of Fort Stevenson and of being directed to his quarters. There I presented the mail and dispatches to Colonel De Trobriand, whom I remember as a portly man with a pleasant face.

After resting a day or two I turned my back on the lower river and started on the return trip. It was a long way to Mike's stockade, but I made it late at night, for I knew that there I would find hay for my horse and a welcome for myself.

I found there a hunting party of Arikara under the leadership of Bloody Knife, a noted hunter and warrior. In the face of danger he was a good man, and in later years lost his life along with Charley Reynolds on that ill-fated day in June, 1876, along the Little Big Horn River when Major Reno, hard pressed, gave the order to retreat, leaving the advance scouts to shift for themselves. His followers were young men and all were garbed in regulation costume, black blanket leggings, breechclouts, calico shirts, and blankets.

These young men talked of their hunting trips and invited me to join them on the next big hunt. Seated on the floor around the fireplace in that rude cabin they told of an exciting chase after buffaloes where they had driven a herd down a walled ridge to a precipice, and though many perished large numbers turned and charged through the ranks of their pursuers.

In the morning the Arikara rode into the hills after game and I bade Mike good-by, little thinking that I would be back again in a few hours minus my horse. It was a pleasant winter morning as I rode along the trail through the cottonwoods to the open prairie, which was really the river bottom land with bluffs on one side and thick brush and cottonwood at a distance, above which could be seen cedar brakes and bluffs on the opposite bank.

After riding four or five miles I came to a point where the timber and the bluff met, leaving a space of a few yards through which the trail wound. Just as I was about to turn a point of the bluff I saw two Indians coming from the opposite direction. On seeing me they at once dismounted and apparently sat down beside a large cottonwood tree that stood near the trail. This did not strike me as unusual, as Indians often get down to smoke and chat when meeting friends on the road. Nevertheless, I drew my gun out of its case and checked the speed of my horse. When I had approached within about twenty or thirty yards they suddenly rose and fired at me, one with a shotgun and the other armed with a bow and arrow. At the same instant I dropped from my nag and fired quickly at the Indian, who was running to the brush for cover. He never got a chance to empty the remaining barrel of his gun, for as he ran I fired at him without taking sight as far as I know, and he dropped. I had no idea that I had hit him, for it was a common ruse for an Indian to drop at the shot, and the brush concealed him. The uncertainty that he might pop up at any moment in my rear was a very disturbing factor during my engagement with his companion.

At the outset, when the Indian fired at me my horse plunged, but I was already on the ground. I felt that he was hit, and later perceived that he had joined the other two horses. Now ensued a duel with the remaining Indian, who had quickly taken station behind the big cottonwood tree. I do not mind confessing that this duel had little charm for me. My opponent did not appear to have a gun, but from his vantage point behind the tree he would shoot an arrow at me whenever the opportunity presented itself. I had the bluff behind me, while for a background the Indian had the forest. Neither of us could retreat without presenting a mark for the other to shoot at, but I kept backing away step by step.

I think it must have been while I was dismounting that an arrow was sped which grazed the skin above my right knee, for it occasioned but a slight, dull pain, which at first I scarcely noticed. The warrior had a fancy for exhausting my ammunition, for he would stick out his robe in the most enticing manner on both sides of the tree and the moment my bullet shivered the bark, like a flash he would discharge an arrow. But his every action, which I closely watched, gave me the cue as to the proper moment or movement to dodge the arrow so that presently, as I backed away, my course led me to where arrows were sticking in the ground on each side of my trail. This was kept up for some time. Once, as I held the carbine poised ready to take aim, he watched me out of his snake-like eyes, and I had a good look at his malignant, treacherous face. He had a piece of wolf-skin wrapped round his head, and his body was hidden beneath his fine silky robe. Whenever I took aim he retired within himself, as it were, behind the tree. I was cool enough, my chief anxiety being in regard to the situation of the other Indian, who had disappeared at the shot, also the possibility that these two might be the advance of a war party. "Who are you?" I demanded, once during an interval. "Oglala me," he replied, but to further questioning he made no answer.

KELLY'S DUEL WITH TWO SIOUX WARRIORS

From an illustration by C. M. Russell, in "Back-Trailing on the Old Frontiers."

Carrying the Mail

I fell to studying the movements of his robe as he stuck it out to attract my fire and finally I managed to break his arrow arm by a well-directed shot. He rushed toward me in fury and despair, attempting, meanwhile, to place an arrow on the string of his bow, but I dropped him in his tracks. During the encounter my horse had joined the Indian ponies and the three animals were working around the point of hill out of sight. In the hope of detaining my mount I fired at one of the Indian ponies before they were lost to sight. I was not disturbed at the thought of being set afoot so much, for I was young and lusty and could make nearly as good time on foot as I could mounted, but the horse belonged to the government and I was accountable for him.

The Indian lay sprawled at my feet, dead. I surveyed the situation and listened for sounds, for I was obsessed with the fear that there was a war party close by. I knew that not far up the river was the camp of friendly Indians with whom I had stayed on my way down. I longed for company. At last I turned and made for the stockade camp of Red Mike as fast as I could travel, looking back every moment expecting to see a bunch of mounted Indians in pursuit.

On reaching the stockade I surprised the hunter with my tale, and his first act was to close and bar the heavy gate, the only entrance to the cabin. Presently Bloody Knife and his friends appeared on the scene, for it seems that they had heard the shooting from the hills, and I had to tell my story over again. At first they were mystified, but suddenly as with one impulse they jumped on their ponies and galloped up the trail. Half an hour later we descried them coming down the trail singing and waving from long coup-sticks what looked suspiciously like scalps. They were in a great hurry to go back to the main camp at Fort Berthold, and paused only long enough to say that they had found the warrior with the shotgun in the place where I had dropped him, shot through the thighs.

The Arikara were not scared, but they wanted to get away from the neighborhood. I thought it strange that they brought away nothing but scalps. I afterward learned that as Bloody Knife and his companions approached the main camp of the associated Mandan, Arikara, and Grosventres at Fort Berthold they rode around in circles, firing their guns and shouting a pæan of victory, and waving the scalps aloft. According to Indian etiquette it is not the man who kills the enemy that counts the victory, but the one who first touches him with hand or coup-stick.

When I had bathed my knee I proposed to Mike that we visit the battle ground and secure the trophies that I had had no time to collect. We found one Indian lying on his face near the cottonwood, minus his scalp. I removed his robe, his bow and quiver containing four arrows, and his belt, knife, and sheath. We then proceeded to the other Indian, who was lying on his face, scalped. The double-barrel shotgun with which he had paid his compliments to me on first acquaintance was a very good one for a trade gun, and it still had a load of slugs in one barrel. I removed his robe, an extra pair of moccasins, a small sack of pemmican mixed with pounded dried cherries, his belt, and a "possible" sack containing sinew for mending, and his powder horn and some broken pieces of lead. I also brought away the picturesque strip of wolf-skin that adorned the head of the bowman.

Early the following day we saw a party of Indians

approaching along the trail in single file. When they came close, we recognized them as friendly Grosventres. They were all old fellows and on being admitted to the cabin sat in silence for some time in a circle on the floor. Finally, one old fellow, with a gesture in the direction from which they had come, spoke one word, and Mike, who understood, pointed to me. Thereupon the Indian got up and shook hands with me solemnly, as did all in turn without a word. They then produced a long pipe and filling it with a mixture of *chashasha* and pulverized plug tobacco, the old fellow who carried the pipe lighted it with a coal from the fireplace and took a few reverent whiffs, during which he pointed it toward the sky and the earth and to the rising and setting of the sun. He then handed the pipe to his neighbor, and it made the rounds of the circle until it was dead. They did not ask for details, nor was there need for them, for the story of the fight was written on the ground like a pictograph on the under side of a buffalo robe. Mike made them some coffee, and after smoking again and shaking hands all round they departed as silently as they had come.

On reaching Fort Buford I reported to the commanding officer and found that the story of the fight had preceded me by Indian runners and that I had acquired some notoriety for killing single-handed two hostile Indians.

CHAPTER IV

A JOURNEY TO FORT PECK

HAVING made my report to the commanding officer, I was the recipient of much commendation on the part of officers and civilians, who one and all wanted to hear the details of my encounter with the two redskins who had endeavored to count coup on a lone white man. Among the officers was Lieutenant Cusick, who was so enthusiastic over the outcome of my adventure that he wished to present me with a fine military overcoat of army blue.

He, also, had had an adventure with the hostiles. The frequent appearance of war parties in the vicinity of Fort Buford made it necessary to send out reconnoitering parties. One day Lieutenant Cusick, who was himself a full-blooded Indian, a member of one of the tribes of the Iroquois confederacy, became separated from his detachment and ran into a small war party; the hostiles, knowing his Indian blood, chased him back to his command, meanwhile whipping him over the head with their bows.

The two lost mail carriers soon returned safely to Fort Buford by a roundabout route and Parshall took me over to the camp of Ed Lambert, the post interpreter. He was a Canadian voyageur of the old school, a man of great muscular strength. It was said that he had once, on a wager, packed on his back a heavy keg of pork around the stockade of old Fort Union.

Lambert spoke fairly good English, and he greeted us with the effusiveness of a Frenchman. His cabin was

ED LAMBERT

JOHN GEORGE BROWN   "YELLOWSTONE KELLY"

mostly kept by his amiable squaw wife and their two half-grown girls. I found him an honest, likable fellow, and he later became a good friend to me. We presently sat down to a repast of buffalo meat, coffee, and hot biscuit. I noticed that on a side table reposed part of a hind quarter of buffalo from which the visitor might carve thin slices of raw meat, which were made palatable by the addition of pepper and salt.

I mentioned the Yellowstone and Lambert said: "Wait until the warm spring weather and I will go with you. We camp in the woods where the timber is to the bank of the plain and we see the antelope 'at feed close by, she look up and around then falls to feed again. Here and there other antelopes in the sunlight; far off, buffaloes."

Before long a band of semi-hostiles, whose habit it was to go on the warpath when the grass was good, sent in word from the Red Water, across the Yellowstone, that they were coming in to trade and would give an open-air dance for the benefit of the military. True to their notice, they soon trooped in, men, women, and children, as befits a trading party, and halted in front of the post trader's store, turning their horses loose under guard along the prairie.

These Indians were mainly Yanktonai, but I fancy there was among them a sprinkling of Teton and Oglala from other camps, out for a good time. Under the direction of a sort of Indian major-domo they ranged in a circle, stripped to breechclout and leggings, and adorned with brass and silver ornaments, paint, and feathers. Suddenly at the sound of an Indian drum thirty or forty of them commenced to dance to a monotonous chant in which they all engaged, shuffling, bowing, and

turning in most grotesque fashion. Although the
weather was cold they did not seem to mind the expo-
sure. In one dance the women joined, and though they
merely hopped about in clumsy fashion their voices
joined melodiously with the deeper voices of the warriors.

In another the men were garbed in buffalo robes
with the hairy side out. They presented a picturesque
appearance, some of their movements simulating the
advance and retreat of a band of buffaloes; now they
appeared confused, then, rendered desperate, they suddenly charged, and so on. I had reason to remember
these counterfeit buffaloes later on when Sandy and I
were stalked by a war party similarly habited, near the
Bear Paw Mountains in Montana.

Officers, enlisted men, civilians, and Assiniboin stood
at a little distance to view these dances, and in return
were keenly scrutinized by the dancing warriors.

Meanwhile, the trader had provided materials for a
feast, consisting of a liberal supply of flour, coffee,
sugar, and bacon, which the squaws soon cooked over
their camp fires. After the repast was finished the warriors traded some fine buffalo robes and other skins for
more coffee, sugar, and flour, and loading up their ponies departed up river.

Some time after this affair a war party appeared before the fort and fired a few shots at the horse corral.
Being pursued hotly by the soldiers and friendly Indians, they plunged into the Missouri, although the ice
was still running, and swam across hanging to their
horses' tails. One of the friendly Indians captured a
horse and led it in triumph before the assembled camp

while some old squaws capered about, chanting a song in praise of his achievement.

In advance of this event, becoming weary of inaction, I had taken a pony and sled and crossed the river on the ice, leaving a trail in the fresh snow that could be seen for a mile.

A short distance up the Yellowstone a small gulch comes in on the left. Prowling along this gulch I came upon an elk making tracks to the north. I shot him, and after dressing the carcass, finding it too late to return to the fort, I loaded it on the sled and made for the woods near by. There I spread the elk skin on the snow and lying down on it, wrapped in my blankets and with a good robe over me, passed a comfortable night. A pack of wolves made a din all night long, but knowing that they never harm a live man I lost no sleep on their account and only regretted that I had not brought a bottle of strychnine along to make medicine for their pelts.

I returned to Buford in a snowstorm and it was well that I crossed the river when I did, for a few days later the warmer waters of the Yellowstone flooded the Missouri and the river broke up, forming a jam that piled the ice cakes high upon the bars and low bottoms, where they remained long after the river and land were clear of winter's gear.

Spring was long in coming and I became restless again; life at Fort Buford seemed unbearably humdrum. To the north lay Fort Peck, a center of trade where Indians came and went, with nothing between but buffaloes and wild life, save the ruins of old Fort Union. Alone, I wandered out there and amid the ruins of the burned stockade and blackened chimneys pictured in imagination the daily scene at Fort Peck; the lookout

"Yellowstone Kelly"

reports a party approaching; they come, and in the camp house receive largess in the shape of tobacco and coffee, and deliberate while the clerks take stock of their robes and skins. After trading they feast, and if other trading parties chance along together they wear out the night with drum and dance. As I pictured such scenes there rang in my brain the couplet,

> Keep not standing fixed and rooted
> Briskly venture, briskly roam

and I resolved to adventure the unknown trails leading to the north.

Having nothing to pack but my rifle and blankets, I turned my pony loose on the range to take his chance with the herd, for I felt more at home afoot and safer while traversing the friendly woods that bordered the bottom lands of the Missouri.

"Start in the evening, boy; the Indians watch this place," advised Lambert. He also cautioned me not to scare the buffalo, saying: "That is food."

I bade my friends good-by, and, starting in the frosty starlight, traveled until I thought I was near the Big Muddy, where I turned into the woods and made camp. The next morning there were buffaloes in sight on the near-by hills, and I noticed a sentinel bull standing motionless on the tip of a small butte. Bands of antelopes grazed near the herds of buffaloes and I was careful not to disturb them, for they were the eyes of their big, clumsy friends.

I traveled all day, and night had already fallen when I suddenly ran into three lodges right on the trail. All was dark and still. I opened the skin flap that served for an entrance to one of the lodges and across some glimmering coals came a man's voice in greeting, with an invitation to enter. Stepping through the small orifice, I was welcomed by a middle-aged Indian habited in black leggings and breechclout, without shirt or blanket. Pointing to a pile of robes back of the smoldering fire, he proceeded to make a light with dry willows and cottonwood sticks as though he had only been awaiting my appearance for this purpose.

Placing my rifle on the couch behind me, I unslung the small pack I carried, removed my belt and knife, and together with my light mittens, which I wore on a sling across my shoulders, put all with my rifle. No one else was about, but presently three little girls came in and were much surprised to see a stranger. Then a woman appeared, and paying no attention to me busied herself about pots and pans near the entrance. Meanwhile, I explained to my host, who was filling a pipe, that I was on my way to the trading post above. He nodded, then smiled, and made signs that I had left the soldiers' tepee the night before, which set me to wondering if he really knew or was only guessing.

I noticed that there was plenty of meat hanging on light poles suspended across the skin lodge, which was new and well made; also that the filled parfleches contained dried meat. After we had eaten some boiled buffalo meat and smoked together the woman went out and soon after a stout-looking buck came in, and regarding me coldly, asked my host why he harbored one of a race who were not friendly to the Indians, and suggested that he tell me to move on. The elder man by his gestures deprecated such treatment and intimated that it was better to treat the stranger fairly and send him safely on his way, all of which failed to convince my op-

ponent, who departed scowling impatiently. I felt no
immediate concern for I knew that I was safe as long as
I should remain in the camp. After I left it would be
another matter, as I might be followed with hostile
intent.

I was given a warm nest of robes for a bed and I fear
that the little girls suffered from cold in consequence,
for in the night my host got up and made a fire. In the
morning, before I had got ready to resume my journey,
my host busied himself with a small buck-skin pouch
into which he put a couple of handfuls of mixed tobacco
and red willow bark, together with a short-stemmed
stone pipe such as the traders retail, and thrust the
whole into my hands, saying: *"Wasityu! chanda, chashasha, chandopia."* The little Indian maids looked on
with interest.

Not to be outdone in the gift business, I picked up
three little sticks of irregular length, and concealing
them in my hand, signed to the little girls to each draw
one. They held back until the father motioned them to
comply. To the one who drew the longest stick I gave
one of my choicest red blankets, which pleased them all
very much. When I camped that night I filled the pipe
and smoked the mild combination which had been given
me. From that day I gradually acquired the tobacco
habit, which I found soothing and companionable.

Bidding my host good-by, I resumed my journey up
the river, keeping a good lookout for possible trouble
on the part of my surly friend of the night before. Although I saw nothing of him, for the sake of greater
safety before reaching Milk River I left the beaten trail
where it cuts through the open country toward Fort
Peck.

A Journey to Fort Peck

Buffaloes and antelopes were plentiful along my route and tempted me more than once for a shot, but caution held my hand until evening, when, about to camp, I killed an antelope that had strayed from the band into my immediate vicinity. At this season of the year antelope meat is preferable to venison. It has a distinctive odor, differing much from deer, but the meat is sweet and palatable, though a little coarse when fresh. The animal does not take on back fat like a deer; instead the fat is distributed in layers through the meat. Taking some ribs and the liver, I hung the carcass on a limb for whoever might chance to come after me, and turning into the dusky cottonwood forest, found a camping place where I felt reasonably safe for the night.

Fort Peck stood on the high bank of the Missouri opposite the mouth of the Big Dry and commanded a view in three directions. The space between the river and the bluff was so scant at this point that the bastioned stockade almost touched the hill in the rear, while in front there was barely space enough to permit a wagon and team to turn around. It seemed as though the locating authority had approached the site by river steamer, and dismayed by the never-ending bars, shoals, and snags, had decided that the fort should be located on the next high bank that showed itself free from erosion. From the crest of the hill in the rear the view was more extensive. There was but one entrance to the fort, with a stout wooden gate that was locked at night.

The Big Dry was a famous buffalo range and from across the river came Yankton, Teton, Hunkpapa, and Oglala Sioux with loads of buffalo robes and pelts of antelope, deer, fox, wolf, beaver, and sometimes a mountain lion or wolverine. The robes were duly baled in a regular baling press, the other pelts by hand. From the north came Assiniboin and Santee, and lastly the Red River half-breeds with their robes and pemmican.

Anyone was welcome at this post who would be of service in an emergency, and all were free to stay as long as they pleased. There was one table for employees and a later one for the trader and his clerk and such visitors as might happen along.

The Milk River country was one of the best buffalo grounds in the Northwest. While there, I went out repeatedly to hunt. If there are no antelopes near, a hunter can approach very close to a band of feeding buffaloes, and if he can pick out the leading cow can obtain several shots. On one of my hunts I happened to shoot a young leader. The rest were confused for a moment, when another young cow, sizing up the situation, forged ahead in the snow and the others instantly followed, the bulls, less swift, wagging their beards and tagging on behind.

The following winter I spent a few days lower down on Milk River with a veteran wolfer, trapping and hunting. Leaving Ashby's trading post on the lower river, we came to a favorable spot to put out baits for wolves. We found a little bottom on a creek away from the river, where there were a few old cottonwood trees, some dry slabs for wood, and a small platform on which reclined the skeleton of a young Indian with all his paraphernalia about him—a wooden saddletree with the leathers removed, a few dilapidated articles of clothing, an old bow minus a string, a cup, a broken pipe, and some bits of lariat—none of which would pass muster in the happy hunting grounds.

A Journey to Fort Peck

The proximity of departed spirits did not disturb us for we knew that Indians as a rule would avoid the place, or if they saw from a distance our fire at night would hurry by muttering "Okshena Duta has built a fire to warm his bones." We built a lean-to, and put out our traps, also the carcasses of two buffaloes as bait for wolves. Hardly had we completed these preparations when a furious storm overtook us, which lasted for three days. While it lasted we took things easy in our camp. One day a herd of buffaloes drifted down before the gale, which was blowing about fifty miles an hour, and at the same moment we descried a herd of elk breasting the storm along a ridge running parallel with our camp. They made a fine show as they passed, massed in column, kicking up the snow, uncertain, but without fear of the buffaloes in the hollow, who were within their range of scent. I noticed many fine pairs of antlers before they disappeared from view in a whirl of snow.

Meanwhile, the buffaloes were pressing along so close that we were in danger of being run over. At this juncture my partner threw a stick of wood, which hit an old bull on the back. The animal paid no attention to this, and thinking his hide would make a cover for us on a cold night I rose up and plugged him in the center of the mass of hair that hung over his eyes.

I had been told that a .44 caliber Henry bullet would not penetrate the bone through this mass of hair and sand, but he dropped and there was great tumult as the herd parted right and left, slipping, sliding, and falling over each other in their excitement. Skinning him was no fun, but at night the heavy green hide stretched over the canvas that covered our bed kept us snug and warm. When we awoke in the morning we found it had frozen stiff, so that we had to raise it up and push it over like a huge slab.

By the time we had skinned enough wolves to load one pony we concluded to return to Fort Peck, for the incessant firing to the north of our camp indicated that the Indians were killing buffaloes on a big scale, and though they might be friendly their proximity was not at all reassuring.

Above Fort Peck the valley narrows so that the hill and bluffs on both sides almost meet. Higher up the river the ridges were clothed with cedar and here the deer loved to range in winter. I found good hunting here and brought down many a buck and doe until the season advanced, when they began feeding on the pungent berries or branches of the juniper. I also noted wolves, the big timber and buffalo wolves that follow and prey upon all game.

Forming a party of four hunters at Fort Peck under the leadership of an experienced trapper, we left the cedar ridges one morning and turned our horses toward the broken country between the Missouri and Milk rivers. We soon arrived at a convenient ground from which buffaloes could be seen on every hill, but two of our party became dissatisfied or apprehensive of danger and wished to turn back to the Missouri. This state of feeling quickly resulted in a division of the food and supplies. Jimmy Deere, honest friend and steadfast partner, agreed to stay with me if I thought the locality reasonably secure from Indians. The other men departed, leaving us with only one horse to pack our outfit.

Our camp was pitched in a little hollow near a water hole. Spring was approaching and there was very little snow on the ground. About three hundred yards away was a sheltered hillside, where we soon killed an old cow. We quickly ripped her open lengthwise and skinned one side, then running the butcher-knife along the ribs close to the backbone and the inner side of the forequarter we pulled the entire side down flat on the ground and removed the paunch and entrails. The two big hollows thus formed we filled with meat slashed from the ribs, hind quarters, fore quarters, neck, and brisket. To this mess we added the contents of two small vials of strychnine, but before doing so we removed the cow's tongue and marrow bones. Buffalo tongue is very rich eating and roasted marrow bones are not to be despised. Swabbing the mess by hand with a big chunk of meat and rubbing an extra bottle of poison into the slashed parts of the animal, the bait was ready. In cold weather it was customary for the wolf hunter to flag the carcass the first night so as to let it freeze hard and compel the wolves to gnaw slowly; otherwise, a small pack of wolves would devour a bait in one sitting.

Nothing bothered our bait the first night, and the following day we put out a couple more buffaloes higher up the rocky little valley, which was bare of shrubs and vegetation. The next morning on getting up Jimmy exclaimed: "The bait has been moved; it is not in the place where we left it." Sure enough, it was on another little side hill. It did not seem possible that anything short of a team of horses could have dragged it down into the gulch and up the hill where it now lay. We hastened toward it and when we arrived about half way we perceived what had really happened. A big cinnamon bear had tackled our bait, dragged it down to the hollow out of observation, and having gorged himself had gone to sleep on the hillside, where we mistook him for our bait.

Our program did not contemplate poisoning bears for they, being fat, were supposed to be immune. Moreover, with our meager transportation facilities weight was a consideration, and wolf-skins were more valuable, pound for pound, than bear. However, the hide proved an asset in more ways than one. Our pony had a sore back, and when we placed the hide on his back, skin side down, the baptism of grease hastened the healing process. The animal's fur was in good condition and we utilized the skin to soften our bed, for there was nothing else suitable for this purpose within reasonable reach.

The buffaloes had not been disturbed by our invasion of their natural feeding ground and, as usual, I saw bulls on the extreme points of buttes, like so many sentinels. One old bull took a roll near our camp, kicking up his heels like a horse, and I am not sure but he rolled over, which he might easily have done by giving his heels the proper twist and the muscles of his back the right swing.

Two days later we went to our advanced baits to skin the wolves and having finished had returned but a short distance when we heard a shot in the hills. This gave us some concern, yet we did not hasten our footsteps. On reaching our camp we tied the horse in a little hollow a few yards away and ate a cold lunch, at the same time keeping a good lookout; we then disposed our things in the best manner for defense and waited to see what would happen. Before long we descried at some distance a line of Indians afoot, following in single file the tracks we had made in returning to camp. As they approached

A Journey to Fort Peck

I saw that each man had his weapon in hand, ready for use, and turning to Jimmy, said: "I will do the talking."

I could not talk much but I could make signs. There were twelve or fourteen in the party, all men excepting one boy. Most of them wore robes with the skin side out; some had blankets, all with a belt or thong tied round the waist allowing the top part to hang down, while across their shoulders were suspended buckskin or elk sheaths for their arms.

They were now coming along on a hot trail, confident that they were nearing their quarry. When I thought them close enough we rose from behind the rocks that formed our shelter, and displaying our arms, I signed to them to halt. With one voice they cried out: "Dakota!" and returning their bows and guns to their sheaths, advanced smiling and grinning.

As soon as they spoke I knew that they were Assiniboin, for their accent was different from that of the Yankton and Teton Sioux, who also call themselves Dakota. The Assiniboin, as we knew them on the American side of the boundary line, were not a warlike people, although they had some husky warriors. They were at peace with the Sioux and were also on friendly terms with their nearest neighbors on the north, the prairie Grosventres.

They laughed and pointed at the pony in the hollow and called for tobacco, producing a long-stemmed redstone pipe. I gave them a piece of plug from the supplies left us by our late comrades. By this time they were all seated on the ground. The man with the pipe quite deliberately cut the tobacco into fine particles, and mixing it with larb, thrust part of the mixture into the pipe, tamping it in with a round piece of wood the size of a lead pencil, which he carried for that purpose. I took a puff and then passed the pipe to Jimmy, who in his turn sent it on around the circle, the fragrant larb filling the air like burning incense.

The partisan, as they call the leader, informed me that they had come from Milk River, that the women and children were now en route to the trading post by the travois trail, and that they had many skins and robes loaded on ponies and dogs. I asked him if travois were used on dogs. "Yes," he said, "and they carry two robes and sometimes a papoose." When they found that they could not separate us from a piece of bacon (which they prize mostly for the salt and fat) or some coffee, they got up, shook hands, and struck out in the direction of Fort Peck.

We also made preparation to leave. I had observed the Indians glancing at the pony and I knew that he had once belonged to these people but had changed hands several times. He might change hands again if they found him unwatched, for the poor animal had to feed some distance from camp in order to find subsistence. He had been a buffalo horse. That meant swiftness to overtake cows and to swerve lightly after the shot to protect his rider.

We could not carry all of our plunder, but we packed the pony and after dark started for the cedar ridges bordering the Missouri. We did not go far, for we stumbled onto a small bank of snow on the shady side of the ravine where there was some grass, and camped.

Next morning we were up bright and early, and soon were traversing the fragrant cedar ridges, now much tracked with deer sign.

Wanting some deer meat, I now took the lariat from

A Journey to Fort Peck

Jimmy's hand, and leading the horse, forged ahead with mind and eye intent upon a bunch of deer retiring slowly from the trail in front, while my companion kept watch on all sides a little way back. Suddenly a shot rang out close behind me and turning I saw immediately behind the pack horse a large mountain lion lying across the trail, dead without a quiver.

I will let my companion tell how this happened, as he related it when we reached the trading establishment: "Kelly was ahead leading the pony and stooping down, for there were deer almost within shot, when I saw this mountain lion about three yards from the trail, crouched and ready to spring. Seeing that my partner had not noticed him and fearful that the lion would strike him or the pony, I fired; at the shot he sprang into the air, and when he landed on the trail he was already dead."

Of course the lion was watching the deer when I disturbed him, and being in a stooping position, he was not alarmed and perhaps had a notion to attack, but I think that the squeaking of the leathers on the pack saddle made him pause and then Jimmy's bullet struck him.

Loosing the lariat halter from the pack horse so that he could nibble the slender herbage of the ridge, we stood for a moment admiring the supple proportions of the lion as he lay relaxed in the repose of painless death. Then we removed his hide and passed on. Descending the ridges, we came to the Missouri and had a refreshing drink of its wholesome water, than which there is no better when free of the sediment that comes with the June flood.

We made an early camp in a wood and stretched some of our skins to keep their shape and lighten our load. Though we did not kill a deer we nevertheless had a feast at this camp for we brought with us a couple of marrow bones clothed in meat, a length of intestine, and a marrow gut.

I prepared the principal dish, which consisted of a stuffing, using the large intestine for a container. Washing this for the second time, I turned it inside out and washed it again. Then I tied one end with a bit of sinew. It was now ready to be filled. Cutting bits of buffalo meat and adding some bits of bacon to give it body, I mixed a little of our precious flour and made some tiny dumplings which went in with the meat until the container was properly full, then I tied the end and laid the whole on a bed of live coals and watched it cook. It lost shape rapidly and had a tendency to curl, making it difficult to manage, but it cooked without a break; the marrow bones, meanwhile, were browning, and when ready needed only a tap with the back of a butcher-knife to break in two and reveal the richness within.

My masterpiece was now not at all attractive in appearance, but when cut in two and shared each particular morsel was a delight, and with the marrow and a cup of coffee fulfilled the requirements of a square meal.

CHAPTER V

EXPLORING THE YELLOWSTONE

IT was in the month of May, close on to June, that Chagashape, "Worker of Wood," as the Indians called Lambert because he was handy with an ax, gathered his things together and bidding good-by to his family, indifferent to the reproaches of his wife for "going off on such a fool trip," said, "Hurrah, boy, the sun is soon quit; let us go."

The trail led through a long stretch of cottonwood timber to a point on the Missouri opposite the mouth of the Yellowstone where I had left a light skiff, with which we entered the river, avoiding the shifting whirlpool that sucks with a strong eddy where the two rivers meet. At this point, where the land is bare of timber or brush, there stood a stout post of cottonwood with a crotch, and a couple of old buffalo skulls lying at its foot. I fancied that an Indian scaffold had once stood there and I asked Lambert about it.

He said that many years before a fight had occurred on that bottom between a war party of Crows and the Sioux, and a chief was killed. He did not remember whether it was a Crow or a Sioux, but a low scaffold was erected and on this rude platform the body, wrapped in a fine robe, was placed, together with the arms and other equipment considered necessary to furnish the ghostly abode of dead warriors. Over all was placed a stout skin lodge of the regulation type, poles, smoke fenders, and entrance flap.

This landmark stood for many years. Gradually the

sinews and thongs that held skin and framework rotted and fell apart. Storms scattered the light gear and the wood decayed until nothing was left but the stout crotch and the buffalo skulls at its foot.

Into the current we paddled our light craft, up and around Snaggy Bend, where the channel was infested with sharp snags into which the current drove; but we, skirting the shallows with difficulty, soon left the whirling waters behind. As the shadows of evening deepened, we halted beside a sloping bank and made our camp close to where a family of beavers had a nest under the bank. In the moonlight we could see their dark noses pointing swiftly up and down stream, leaving a V-shaped wake behind. When alarmed, or in play, they would strike the water with their flat tails, making a loud noise as they disappeared, only to reappear at a distance and repeat the operation.

In the morning we pulled our boat several miles up the river to a timbered bank, beyond which lay a broad expanse of prairie that extended to the distant hills to the northward, rich land covered with buffalo and bunch grass. Here we cached our boat, for we did not intend taking it farther. We made a temporary camp and then went to take a survey of the prairie.

It was a beautiful place and view. The smooth bottom land was turfed to the edge of the timber, to which the bank, six feet higher than the bottom, sloped. It was an ideal spot for a camping ground, but Lambert opined that Indians did not camp here for the reason that for some distance the river bank was not suitable for watering stock, as shown by the absence of game or buffalo crossings. Within one hundred yards of us two beautiful creatures, antelopes, were quietly grazing. Many more were to be observed out on the flat, while beyond them grazed a small herd of buffaloes.

Your prong-horn is a graceful animal. If you show yourself suddenly he will turn and look, then dance away, or perhaps circle around and stop again, for he has great curiosity, and if you lie down and flap your arms or legs vigorously he may come within gunshot. In winter the ankles of the front feet are often a mass of prickly pear thorns, but this does not inconvenience him for he has been equipped by nature to seek the protection of areas of cactus when pursued by wolves or coyotes, who halt suddenly on the edge of a cactus patch. He also stamps the cactus to get at the tender grass. The mother antelope conceals the newly born in such places. I found one once, well grown, and caught it with a view of making it a pet, but coming along to a wayside cabin in the Judith Basin, I learned of the tragedy of the Custer battlefield of a few days earlier and leaving the young antelope with the man in charge, turned my horse toward the Yellowstone country.

Lambert and I wanted an antelope that day very badly, but we would not kill one of the two so close to us because the shot might alarm the buffaloes out on the plain; so we wandered up the stream a couple of miles and keeping close to the timber, out of observation, killed a two-year-old, skinned and cleaned it, and suspended the carcass on a tree, where the drying winds soon formed a glaze on the meat which prevented the blow flies from getting in their work.

On we went, sometimes in the timber and then again skirting the prairie, but saw no deer or elk, they being, as we surmised, higher in the gulches and ridges. Beaver sign was abundant, their yards in the water being jammed with white-peeled sticks of cottonwood on which they feed, the strong odor of their castors filling the air.

We returned to the place where our boat was cached, and building a small fire toward evening cooked some antelope meat and boiled a few potatoes that Lambert had raised and stored in a cache in the Mandan style. After we had eaten of the meat and potatoes and refreshed ourselves with a cup of coffee, we sat and talked while the fire sank to a bed of coals. I wish I could remember some of the tales of adventure that Lambert delighted to relate, so that I might recount them here with the accuracy they deserve, but I can now recall only one, that happened at Fort Peck when Lambert was interpreter and trader.

Sitting Bull was among the noted Sioux leaders who frequented the buffalo ranges between the Yellowstone and the Missouri, for the region lay on the line of movements of big game and was also convenient to the Fort Peck trading establishment, as well as for forays on the Crow, Piegan, and Blackfeet north of the Missouri. They could also kill a white man occasionally and lay it to their enemies. The Red River people, also, had their camps in the Milk River country, where rum might be obtained for furs and horses. For all these reasons the region was much resorted to by many bands of Sioux, and later by their allies, the Cheyenne.

Sitting Bull, being somewhat of a prophet and medicine man as well as a warrior, attracted restless spirits from all tribes, and though his immediate following might consist of a few families he had the nucleus of a good-sized war party. Crossing the river at Fort Peck with his gang of cutthroats, he demanded that the goods

RAIN-IN-THE-FACE
Courtesy General Nelson A. Miles.

SITTING BULL
Courtesy Museum of the American Indian.

store be opened for trade. When this was done he went behind the counter and said, "I will show you white men how to trade with Indians." He measured cloth and dealt out sugar, coffee, flour, powder, caps, and ammunition to his followers in exchange for furs and skins in proportions which he deemed fair and just, while Lambert walked up and down past an open keg of powder, smoking his pipe, ready to blow up the store if things went to extremes. Even a savage would think twice, however, before destroying the most prominent trade store in the country, so they cooled down and finally went their way after setting fire to several ranks of cordwood piled on the river bank.

Lambert and I made preparations for an extended trip up the river afoot if we found things quiet and no fresh Indian sign. Caching the greater part of our stuff we traveled light, stopping where we had hung the antelope to cut the meat in thin slabs for frying, taking care to tie a white rag to keep off the birds. Past the lignite vein of coal exposed on the opposite bluff with its curious slope, past some rapids and shoals, we finally came to the neighborhood of a creek where Glendive is now located. Above that point, convenient to the river we killed a bull and a fat cow. Skinning the animals carefully, we cut up the meat for drying, arranged it on poles, and set about making frames of willow for two bull boats.

After the green skins had been tied on to the frames they were left to dry and we traveled farther up the river. There were some bluffs on the south side that we wanted to examine for mountain sheep, but we concluded that it might be unsafe to wander so far from the river, not knowing how close we would get to camps or hunting parties whom it was the part of wisdom to avoid. The valley had narrowed so that there was almost no plain, and the swift current indicated that more rapids were near. Finding there was better cover on the south bank, we made shift to tie together a raft of driftwood with willows, a work at which Lambert proved to be quite skilful. Crossing over, we advanced to where there was open country ahead, and just before us the fresh skeleton of a sweat wickiup built of newly peeled willows, showing a recent occupation, and a well-worn trail down the bank across to the opposite sand bar, where many horses had passed. There was no concealment anywhere but the bank under which we were.

Looking over the bank, we saw five mounted Indians heading directly for us on the trail. A few yards below us a broken point of the bank projected a little and to this we ran, hoping that the Indians would cross without observing us. They rode down the bank, and taking the ford without stopping, their attention was occupied for a moment in keeping their horses on the course; on getting into shallow water they saw us, and scattering, circled around on the sand bar, but seeing no hostile movement on our part, one of them who recognized Lambert called him by his Indian name, demanding his business in the Indian country.

Lambert answered in Sioux, saying: "We have been hunting and are now on our way home."

This did not satisfy the speaker and he asked: "Where is the rest of your party, and what people are they?" To which Lambert shouted, "Go on, go on; when you come to our house to trade for goods do we ask you questions?"

They had kept their horses moving all this time,

though not increasing their distance from us, and on these words they holloed loudly and would not listen to Lambert's further remarks. They moved off slowly and when they had attained what they considered a safe distance indulged in some insulting gestures. They had another channel of the river to cross, and we watched them as they climbed the farther bank and low bluff. There they dismounted and consulted among themselves, apparently, while regarding us. Then they led their horses over a rise and disappeared from view.

Lambert said that they were Oglala and a mean lot. We, also, held a hasty consultation, the result of which kept us on the course we were pursuing until we reached the mouth of a deep gulch, up which we turned as far as the low cedar hills and worked our way down the country parallel with the river to a point opposite the place where we had tied the raft, which we managed to reach without further incident and, as we believed, unperceived.

Getting aboard, we used poles for paddles in keeping the unwieldy craft in mid-stream and dropped to the lower end of the bend, where we tied it up again for use in a possible emergency and took to the tall timber. It was not until the next day that we reached our bull boat camp, which had not been disturbed. The boats were not more than half dry, neither was the meat, which we hastened to turn over on the poles so as to give the other side a chance to cure. We liked this camp, and having taken all due precaution, felt that we could camp for a day, or two days if necessary, to dry the boats and the meat sufficiently to lighten our loads. After a trip to the prairie to see if everything was serene, we carried the heads and bones of the two buffaloes to a bunch of brush and removed traces of the killing as much as possible. From the edge of the prairie numerous antelopes were seen feeding quietly, but the number of buffaloes had increased greatly so that they covered the far extent of the plain and the hills beyond.

Lambert surmised that the Indians had been hunting them on the south side of the river and when the buffaloes crossed had followed leisurely and made camp at some distance from their feeding grounds, as usual, and would probably resume the chase when the camp got short of meat and skins. This was the season when they made new lodges and parfleche, and leather for footwear and other uses.

The scene was exhilarating; the dark bodies of the buffaloes as they moved in clusters or singly, the combative bulls raising a dust cloud as they came together, contrasted with the light-colored antelopes on the outskirts, ready to give alarm at a moment's notice.

It was said that wolves killed more buffaloes than the Indians and whites combined. I am convinced that the men engaged in poisoning wolves for their pelts rendered a good service in protection of herds of wild game. I have seen in the North bands of wolves numbering fifty or more traveling with noses up on the scent of buffaloes borne by the wind. They killed the young calves and hamstrung the cows and bulls. On the other hand, the Indians were very wasteful of the buffaloes. The rapid and continuous firing that we heard when camped by the bier of Okshena Duta near Milk River was caused, I learned later, by Indians killing cows for the unborn calves for purposes of feasting, the cows being at that time of year poor in flesh and the robes by no means prime.

Exploring the Yellowstone

When Lambert and I started on this pilgrimage the probability of meeting hostile Indians was considered and we agreed to avoid conflict, if possible, and if compelled to fight to go the limit according to the occasion. The five Indians whom we met would never tackle two white men on their guard, and even if they succeeded in taking us unaware they would still reckon on some avenue of escape. We had been lucky so far and had had a good time—always a little camp fire at night—because we took precautions. Now we must take still greater precautions for the Indians now knew that at least two white men were in their country disturbing the buffaloes, or spying around for some purpose, and must be hunted out.

We had no desire to play hide and seek, after the manner of Cooper, with these crafty fellows who were buffaloes one minute and yelling savages the next, so while Lambert fried some meat and boiled coffee I stood guard with my rifle in the twilight at the edge of the prairie, intent to see any strange movement of man or beast and listening for any sound or stir that might smack of hazard. We ate our supper by the light and warmth of the dying cottonwood coals that preserve their redness longer than most woods, then rolled in our blankets and went to sleep, leaving no one on guard, for the Sioux do not attack at night.

Before daylight we were up and spent an hour or so looking around. Finding everything quiet, we packed the bull boats through the woods to the water's edge. We loaded our meat and stuff in the smaller boat and putting some skins and blankets together with our arms in the larger, got in and pushed off into the stream. You use a short paddle in propelling a bull boat and this is done by reaching straight out and pulling the paddle toward you. No great progress is made, but it is a safe craft, riding a few inches in the water and rolling around any obstruction it meets, unless it be a tree at right angles to the current.

The friendly deer, and even antelopes, gazed at us undismayed from the sand bars and banks where they had come down for water in the early morning, while elk were plentiful in the willows that fringed the bars. Where the river touched long reaches of prairie we stopped to look for possible enemies. About noon a hasty meal was cooked in a bend of the woods and we continued our journey.

The next day or the following one we reached the place where our skiff was concealed. Here we stayed long enough to kill an elk and a deer, the meat and skins of which were quickly distributed to our various craft, which in motion now assumed the appearance of a small flotilla. With the skiff in the lead our progress was more rapid down stream and with better purchase the skiff's paddles enabled us to race the current, for, as Scott's hero remarks: "even a haggis, God bless her, can charge down hill."

Reaching Snaggy Bend, we had to employ more caution, and taking possession of the larger bull boat, I turned the other adrift and slid around the snags without accident. We landed in front of Fort Buford and had our bull boat, meat, and baggage conveyed on a Red River cart to Lambert's house, where the array of food and skins cheered the hearts of the inmates and their many friends and relatives, who made heavy inroads upon the hospitality of these good people, who never turned anyone away from their table as long as they had a bite to offer.

Three men with whom I had some acquaintance lived in a cabin on the west side of the Missouri a few miles above the Big Muddy, which comes in from the east about thirty-five or forty miles above the mouth of the Yellowstone. In the early fall of 1869 I paid them a visit. Their cabin, which stood on the bank of the river, was built of green logs, cool in summer and snug in winter. The floor was of tough clay and the pinned pole roofing was covered with a layer a foot thick. In one corner was a stone fireplace and chimney. There were three wooden bunks and a gunrack, while some robes, skins, and traps constituted the movable property in sight. There were no port holes in this cabin, but it had two small windows on either side at about the height of one's eyes.

Behind the cabin a forest of heavy cottonwood and willows extended to the bluff about half a mile distant. Beyond this lay the country of the Sioux, the Sans Arcs, and the Teton, to the Musselshell and the upper reaches of the Missouri, where the mountain Crows and prairie Grosventres resorted. In the timber, white-tail, and along the bluff, black-tail deer thronged, while beyond grazed antelopes and buffaloes. Beaver were numerous in the river and at night they could be seen puffing along like miniature steamboats, leaving a broad wake behind.

Truly these men courted danger, engaged as they were in cutting cordwood for the river steamboats plying to Fort Benton, the head of navigation, and to intermediate points. This work they regarded as a side issue to obtain ready money, along with their hunting and trapping.

As it turned out they were more fortunate than a party of four men, new to the country, who had been landed a year or two before at a bank a few miles above by the up-river steamboat, where they built a cabin of rough logs and covered it loosely with slabs and an earthen roof.

One evening a war party encamped near by, and an adventurous warrior stole away in the night to investigate. Concealing himself at a corner of the cabin near the door with his bow and arrows ready for a shot, he waited patiently for a victim. Before long a white man came out for some purpose and the Indian promptly transfixed him with an arrow. This was followed instantly by a second arrow, which he held under his hand on top of the bow, the first arrow being on the string.

In the morning the Indians maneuvered to attract the attention of the inmates to one side of the cabin while the main party approached on the other side. Seizing the muzzles of the white men's guns protruding from the port holes, they pulled down the loose and heavy split timbers of the roof onto the men below, whom they soon dispatched, and when the boat returned from up-river nothing remained but blackened walls and mutilated bodies.

I had been out in the hills hunting one day and was packing home an antelope when my attention was called to the actions of a buffalo cow that came tearing frantically down the hill and ran past me into the woods. I walked back along her track to discover what had caused this commotion and saw down the river, where an open bottom began, a spiral of smoke ascending and

78

some ponies grazing. I made for the timber as fast as I could travel with the antelope on my back, and striking a game trail lost no time in getting to the cabin, where I found that one of my companions had also learned of the presence of strange Indians and had been close enough to their camp to get a good look at them.

"I was down at the lower end of the point near the slough," he said, "when I heard the tinkling of the bells on their ponies. From the thick willows I saw that they had stopped. It is a war party, for I saw the leather cases that hold their war bonnets and things. They are not Sioux or Crows. I did not stay any longer."

It was agreed that we would go down after supper and reconnoiter. After filling up on buffalo meat, coffee, and home-made bread Ed remarked that he had not lost any Indians and if we wanted to hunt Indian camps in the night he would hold the cabin.

Frank and I put on our cartridge belts, and picking up our rifles, stepped out into the clearing and made our way silently in the shadow of big trees and across several openings in the direction of the lower point. The timber was full of noises of the night, animals breaking about and beaver in the river thumping the water with their broad tails, making a report that sounded like the popping of a gun or pistol.

In about half an hour we reached the belt of willows that screened the open bottom land just beyond the slough. As we cautiously made our way, muffled sounds came to our ears and soon the tinkling of bells on the ponies, picketed and hobbled, sounded on the night air. It was apparent that these Indians were not aware of their proximity to white men or they would have taken more precautions. They were now chanting a war hymn that sounded weird and wild as it rose and fell on the still night air. The hymn was a prelude to feasting, for it ceased when roasted meat and bones were handed around the circle. We were so close that the odor of burning sagebrush and roasted marrow bones drifted toward us. One fellow had a side of ribs planted in front of him which he removed carefully and with his sheath knife cut off some of the ribs, which he distributed to those on either side. He then called to someone off with the ponies, but without waiting commenced his repast.

Suddenly, behind us in a tree the low hoot of an owl startled us. The Indians stopped eating at once and looked steadily in our direction. We scarcely breathed, for we thought they must surely discover us where we were crouched. Again came the "hoo-hoo-ah!" of the owl, more mournful than before. An Indian got up and went off toward the ponies. Then Mr. Owl left his perch and with a swish of wings was lost in the night. Our curiosity was satisfied and we retired, silently if not gracefully, into the dark shadows of the forest and returned to the cabin.

The incident of the evening did not disturb our slumber and in the morning there came to our shore an esteemed trapper friend, "Missouri," who was a character in his way. For instance, he preferred to travel and trap alone. Were not two a crowd? Did he ever fall out with himself over beaver traps, or where the trail parted? Not at all. Another thing that to our minds awakened mild scorn was the fact that he drank gruel in place of coffee. Otherwise, he was a good fellow, full of that quaint personality one attaches to Pike County. We fed him and broke the news of the war party.

Life did not seem to run in a satisfactory groove as

long as these Indians remained in our neighborhood and the reason thereof unsolved. After due deliberation on this matter, therefore, we sallied forth into the woods and by trails known to us reached the spot of their late encampment, where we found nothing but an empty prairie, a slinking coyote, some piles of bones, and the ashes of their camp fire still warm.

We now decided to climb the hill back of the river, from which a fine view was to be had, as we had no time to follow the tracks that seemed to overrun the flat. When we had done so, finding nothing in sight, we sat down on the grass to smoke and rest. Suddenly a mounted Indian showed himself about five hundred yards away and circled around as though he had just discovered us. I knew that I could come pretty close to that Indian for I had killed an antelope once at about that distance, so I raised the sight on my rifle and fired. Before I could note any result of the shot the ground around the savage was fairly alive with Indians whipping their horses in our direction. On they came in wild disorder, their ornaments of bright metal flashing in the rays of the morning sun, and there was such a flutter of waving plumes and feathers that the sight was altogether thrilling. We did not stop to admire it, however, for so great was our anxiety to reach the protecting line of timber that with one accord we dropped behind the hill and made for cover as fast as our legs would carry us.

I fear that we did not present a pleasant spectacle as we raced downhill in this sudden change of base, but it was good strategy. On the edge of the slough we turned about and faced the war party, which had now divided its force and was streaming out of the coulees on either side. They had a notion of charging us direct, but on our opening fire they scattered, and forming a thin line, charged past our position, delivering their fire as they passed. The bullets sped over and around us but no one was hit, for the sagebrush afforded us some protection. Our fire was more effective. Missouri tumbled an Indian off his horse and soon there were several riderless animals running about.

One fellow who was riding a white horse paid particular attention to me, and as he rode by like the wind, having already fired at me three times, I pulled down on him as he lay half-concealed along his pony's back plying his whip and shifting his bull-hide shield, and hit the pony instead of the man, which made me sorry, for it was such a fine creature.

While these Indians were drawing our fire several others had dismounted below and were entering the timber. Seeing this movement, I called to my companions to enter the woods. In crossing the slough everyone lost his moccasins except Ed, who wore boots. Entering the willows, we waited for the attack of the Indians, whose shrill cries sounded in different parts of the wood in support and encouragement of each other. We sat in the shadow of a drooping cottonwood, tense and ready for them, eagerly watching for some movement that would afford a mark to fire at, but they contented themselves with a few desultory volleys in our direction as though feeling us out and then all was quiet.

As the war party greatly outnumbered us we looked for them to follow up their advantage, since they had us on the run, but they evidently lacked stomach for it, though I have known three reckless Sioux warriors to follow two white hunters into thick brush, an encounter that ended in a draw of one white man and one Indian. As for us, being barefooted, our ambition for fighting had dwindled to the zero point, and we sympathized with the sentiment of one of our party who had seen more or less fighting in the late war: "I wish I was a baby, and a girl baby at that."

Painfully we made our way across openings and through patches of fire-killed cacti to our cabin, where we found that the Indians had been there before us and had taken everything worth taking, leaving as mementoes of their visit an arrow and a coup lance sticking in the doorway.

Not having any leather for the manufacture of moccasins, we were reduced to most primitive means for a supply of footgear, in which Missouri's little dugout played its part in conveying hunters across the river where game was found and skins obtained. As for myself, I shot a couple of beaver that same night and made a pair of rough shoes which I wore green, keeping them soft in the process of drying by a liberal use of oil and working the skins until they had shaped themselves to my feet. After vainly waiting several days for a steamer, we made our way afoot to Fort Buford for needed supplies.

CHAPTER VI

HUNTING ADVENTURES ON THE YELLOWSTONE

THE three years following the incident just recorded were not especially noteworthy, although full of the incidents relating to the life of a hunter and trapper. My memory is fresh on incidents, but not always with respect to dates or years. As I relate one incident it brings to mind another, happening before or afterward.

On one occasion I traded a rifle and two mountain lion skins to an Indian for a buffalo pony. The Indian had represented the pony as "heap dusa," which means fast. I then started in to hunt buffaloes and once got so close to a bull that I felt tempted to reach out and lay hold of his tail, but thought better of it and bore down on some cows on the edge of a prairie dog village. The animals seemed to sense that I was left-handed for they kept on the right-hand side of the village, which put me at a disadvantage. However, when on clear ground I managed to kill two, one of which made a buffalo robe. The pony was winded after the first run, and no wonder, for he had had to fill his belly by hunting grass under the snow. Soon after this I lost him and never saw him again. No doubt he found his old range across the Yellowstone more to his liking.

In the summer and autumn I made several trips up the Yellowstone; once with Jack Mail, a young man who had hunted in the lower country and was an all-round good fellow and clever hunter. Between trips I read a good deal in books loaned me, and renewed acquaintance with Scott, Poe, and Shakespeare, whose works I had read when I was too young to appreciate fully their value.

One winter I visited a hunting party of Indians who were camped on one of the main branches of the Little Missouri River, near the head of the stream. I remember that it was a very broken country of cedar and pine, where deer and mountain sheep were quite plentiful and not at all wild. It was not far from the rolling plain where buffaloes ranged. It was a new country to me at that time.

There were about forty Indians in the party, two or three of whom were women. They built huts, tepee fashion, of poles and covered them with a thick coat of cedar and pine boughs, and they were very comfortable as long as they were fresh and green. A small fire in the center served to warm the interior and cook the food, which was mostly meat. My little package of tea, coffee, and sugar did not last long, nor did my tobacco, which was in constant demand. "Here," I said, the first night after the shelters were built, "is my supply of tea, coffee, and sugar. Take it. I want it divided and used at once, but the tobacco is another matter; I shall furnish one plug each night as long as it lasts." "How! How!" shouted the assembled hunters, and the pipe man got out his pipe, *chashasha* bag, and little wooden board and tamper, ready for the round circle smoke.

This was in a tepee, much the largest in the camp, but it would not hold all the crowd. I slept in another lodge where the company was more select. In the big tepee people were up all night, smoking and singing, but there was no drum; that was tabooed for some reason, probably on account of the hunt.

As we were in the heart of the game ground, with deer and mountain sheep on all sides, the method pursued was to hunt in a circle. No one was permitted to start until all were ready. At the signal we spread out on all sides as quietly as possible so as to cover some ground before disturbing the game. This usually resulted in a lot of deer being left inside of the circle. The people left in camp got a chance at these when the shooting began.

I took with me a young man who was a near relative of the Mandan youth who on a former occasion had accompanied me from the Mandan village to Painted Woods, on the river below Fort Buford. Our course took us up a fork of the branch we were camped on, and I ran into bunches of black-tail deer and commenced killing them as soon as I heard firing on either side. I very soon had as many down as we could properly handle, and after butchering the animals by removing the entrails and paunch, we turned them over on the snow to drain. They were now ready for those who followed with pack ponies, while we went on to repeat the operation as opportunity offered.

At night there was, of course, great feasting and the air was tainted with the odor of burning bones. I looked for the deer and other game to leave the country, but game was found every day, only farther away. Nothing in the way of meat was wasted, the heads, brains, and some of the intestines passing muster for food, while many pony loads of deer and elk meat were taken to the camps on the Missouri.

This party of hunters was a mixed one and included

86

men of the Mandan, Arikara, and Grosventre villages. I understood from their conversation that the Sioux villages were well to the west of the Yellowstone and that it would be safe to hunt for several days, at least, from the present camp. They held a council each night and laid out the course for the morrow. A watch was kept to prevent surprise, and I saw young men returning with buffalo meat from the plain which extended roughly to the region of Powder River.

When I saw this I wanted to go and get some, also, and broached the subject at a night council. There was silence for a moment while the long flat-stemmed redstone pipe made its rounds. Then one of the leading men, whose name I cannot recall, spoke: "My friend, it is a long way to the buffaloes, and the young men engaged are sent to spy on the enemy and it is no part of their duty to disturb the buffaloes, but when they find one in a coulee they cannot resist trying their arrows. It is best that you do not go."

I was somewhat taken aback, but countered by saying: "If your young men can stand it, I can." But I did not secure the coveted permission. Evidently there was a reason.

I could stand a straight diet of meat for a week or even ten days if necessary, but after that, however rich and palatable the food, I longed for bread and coffee to go with it. I found these hunters agreeable and friendly, but I could not converse with them for I could not talk their language and very few of them could talk Sioux, of which I had acquired a smattering, for it was the language most used by the interpreters and others in their intercourse with the natives; besides, it was easy to learn.

"Yellowstone Kelly"

On the third day I caught my pony from the herd. I had had enough hunting for a while, and my ammunition was running low. I was to get a share of the mountain sheep that had been killed, if it could be sent to Fort Buford. I bade my friends good-by and they all shook hands.

The weather was not cold for late November. I wore at this time a white blanket long coat with hood, and under this a soft buckskin shirt of well-smoked leather. There were no fringes or beads on this shirt, but it had a narrow strip of fur-edged collar and cuffs. I wore moccasins of elk-skin and dark jean trousers, which were encased below the knee. In winter I usually wore a fur cap, either of fox or beaver fur.

On one of our trips up the Yellowstone Jack and I found a bull elk that had been shot the day before. Indians had shot him, but did not have time to follow and finish him. We decided that the skin would be capacious enough for a bull boat, but after removing the hide and sizing it up on some bent willows we concluded otherwise, and pegged it down in a retired spot to dry.

We had already been on the river two days and had secured part of a load of meat. That morning I had spent half an hour approaching an antelope that was very keen-eyed and suspicious, and while running across a bottom to head him off I heard the danger signal of a rattlesnake. I was already in the air, but I made a lightning calculation as to the probability of landing on him, struck ground free, and kept on. The antelope proved to be a very heavy one and was as much as I could pack to camp. On the way a feeling that would not down possessed me that Indians were near and I told my companion we had better get out without delay.

Adventures on the Yellowstone

A serviceable raft was built and our stuff was loaded. In the late afternoon we were at the head of a snaggy bend where a wood camp had been established by a contractor to furnish cordwood for the post, and here we learned that on that very same morning a war party of Sioux had swooped down on some workmen going to the post with wagons and killed two, filling them with arrows, and dispersed the rest. There was supposed to be a guard of soldiers, but the wagons were strung out and the surprise was complete. We luckily escaped contact with that war party, which was said to be a big one, numbering fifty or more.

The following year (I think it was about September or October, 1871) I left the mouth of the Yellowstone mounted on a fine pony that I had traded for, bound for the Milk River country in northern Montana.

Along the upper Missouri at some point between Wolf Point and the Porcupine a river steamboat, the *Amelia Poe,* loaded with a cargo of whiskey and other liquors bound for Fort Benton, had been wrecked on a sand bar some years before. Efforts had been made to remove the machinery and by herculean labor the boiler had been hauled to the top of the high bank, the valuable and small parts being placed in a hole underneath out of reach of Indians who might be tempted to make way with usable steel and brass. The savages had promptly burrowed into this cache, however, and taken what they wanted. The boiler remained a landmark that could be seen some distance.

The shifting of the channel and the encroachment of the sand bar had made it possible for parties to explore the hold of the vessel in search of liquor that it was a sin to lose, and this was the scene that unfolded itself as I rode up one fine morning to survey this old landmark: a fire of driftwood on the sand bar convenient to the river's edge; several men, two of them naked, standing around in its genial warmth; a wagon and camp equipage; and one man with grappling irons up to his neck in the water, feeling with his toes for casks and barrels to fasten to with his grapnel, when those on shore would give a brisk pull on the rope whereupon something would come, it might be a cask of gin or a barrel of whisky.

It sometimes happened that a strong pull would tear the top off the cask and the contents would be spilled in the river. When this occurred it extorted a general wail from the bystanders over the loss of so much good liquor, and they would hasten to revive their spirits from an open dish that stood on a box. I tasted some of it and decided that such whiskey could very well go into the river, though I did not claim to be a judge in that line.

I assume that Major Reed, who had charge of the agency on Milk River, was along to see that no illegal use was made of the salvaged fire-water in his district. I had lunch with the men and renewed acquaintance with the Major, who at that time was in the prime of manhood, punctilious, dashing, and brave, a gentleman of the old school and a fine type of frontiersman. When next I met the Major he had formed a partnership with Bowles and was established in the Judith Basin, Montana, that beautiful region where one could stand in one spot and see buffaloes, deer, elk, mountain sheep, and bears, all at one time. The basin was then a borderland, a disputed ground where Sioux, Crows, and Blackfeet met and exchanged courtesies in the usual savage fashion with clash of arms. This was in the years preceding

Adventures on the Yellowstone

General Custer's advance on the hostile camps along the Little Big Horn, where the Seventh Cavalry met with disaster.

I met the Major again in the little town of Carroll on the bank of the Missouri, above the mouth of the Musselshell, during the retreat of the Nez Percé Indians in the autumn of 1877. I had gone there with Lieutenant Bailey of the Fifth Infantry, accompanied by a small escort of cavalry, across country, and the mission of this officer was to secure a quantity of rifle ammunition which had been left there for military use. Major Reed, it appeared, had locked it for safe-keeping in a small log cabin. We did not know this at the time, and learning where it was stored and not having the key we proceeded to break into the building. The Major came while the soldiers were occupied with this business and was somewhat amused at our antics.

Skimming along the smooth bottoms of Milk River, a day or two after leaving the scene of activity at the wreck of the *Amelia Poe,* and keeping out of the way of the buffaloes and their alert pickets, the antelopes, I came to the spot where I had had an experience with a war party of Sioux the previous spring that I shall not easily forget.

I was traveling afoot bound for Reed's fort. The sun had just risen over the hills as I reached the center of a good-sized flat, when I saw coming over the crest of the rising ground beyond, each particular metal ornament or scheme of fluttering color illumined by the glorious sun, a considerable body of Indians, afoot, strung out in a line at right angles to my course. As they marched slowly down the grassy slope in irregular lines—for more were coming over the crest—with lances and feathers waving, the whole presented a spectacle most striking and war-like. But not for me.

I looked around. It was a far cry to the timber, my mainstay. What was the use? I thought. I could have made it, I presume, for I could run as fast and as far as an Indian, but I felt that I would rather die than be chased like a wolf. There was a rock four or five feet high directly in front. I advanced to this, and taking four or five cartridges out of my pocket held them in my right hand.

The Indians were scattered now, but they came on with that easy, graceful motion of the moccasin wearer, alert and keenly noting, as I suspected, my every motion. When they had approached within one hundred and fifty yards I picked up my rifle and holding it on my right arm ready for use, held up my left arm and made the signal to stop. They halted at once, but after a moment the leader came on ahead. He did not, as I have known them to do on the summons, spread his blanket on the ground and with great ostentation place his arms and sheath knife thereon, but came fully armed, a dignified warrior, with a circlet of bears' claws about his neck and a coil of lariat in his belt, and stood gravely a moment in front of the rock that formed my defense, regarding me while I looked him firmly in the eye. Then with a sweep of his hand to his followers, said, as near as I could understand his words: "Does the *wasityu* hold the road against the Yankton?"

Relieved to hear the speech of the Yankton, which differs slightly from that of the Teton, Brule, Oglala, and other tribes of the Dakota, I answered: "No, let the Yankton come on!" suiting the action with a gesture in

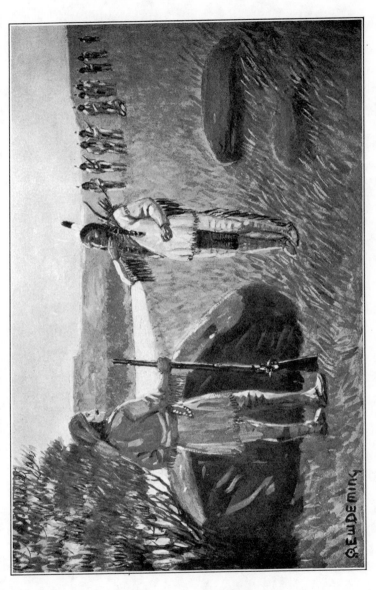

"DOES THE *WASITYU* HOLD THE ROAD AGAINST THE YANKTON?"

the sign language, for the Yankton were not accounted hostile, though there were some hard men among them.

The main party had halted only for a moment and was on the move before I had answered the leader's question, who now, seeing the cartridges that I still held in my fist, placed his hand over his mouth, a sign of wonder, but made no comment. By this time they were all around me, grinning and talking among themselves; the greater part, however, had turned aside toward the river in the direction of the large creeks that come in from the north to the Milk River.

While talking to the leader, to whom I had given a plug of tobacco which I always carried, I learned that this war party had been to the Crow country to steal horses, had fought, and were returning afoot as they had gone out. While we were still engaged in talking a great hubbub arose from the Indians, who were yet only a little way off advancing in an irregular line in the short brush toward the timber. This caused everyone to race with mad speed in the direction of the commotion and I was suddenly left alone.

It was a wild scene, and looking I saw what caused it. A large brown or black bear had been disturbed and was making frantic efforts to escape, in great bounds or a clumsy gallop. He would turn his head first to one side and then to the other in the most grotesque manner. The Indians were seemingly gaining ground when all entered the timber and were lost to view, but I could still hear their cries, mingled with the report of firearms, as the pursuit continued. Though a fairly good sportsman I was not hunting bear that day, although the obtrusion of his bearship at a happier time might have had its effect. I therefore continued my journey, after a delay that seemed an hour or more, but was only a few minutes of stirring life.

And so it was that I came to the scene of a former adventure and reined in my horse beside the rock to survey the prospect about me. The view was different now. The turf was yellow, with that tawny cast of the northern plain. The woods that concealed the meandering river, thinned of their autumn foliage, showed gaps and the yellow hills beyond where well-beaten buffalo trails converged to the crossings.

I traveled on and later in the day struck a fresh lodgepole trail, which presently merged into a party of Assiniboin, bound for some trading post on the upper Milk River. The headman of the village rode in advance, followed by a number of warriors; then came the women leading ponies laden with rolls of skins and tepees, the poles being attached underneath on the saddles with the big ends dragging on the ground. Smaller bundles were carried by some twenty collared dogs atop of poles that were fastened dexterously to the collars and a band that fitted round the hairy animals back of the forelegs. These ran loose along with the ponies and colts on which the small children rode. The rear was brought up by loose ponies, driven by men and boys.

With this cavalcade was an animal that at once attracted my attention. The creature was large for a dog, and had all the actions of a bear, his head and feet only being pure dog. Brown, with short tail and thick fur, he ambled along with the gait peculiar to a brown bear— a very odd specimen.

In early May, 1873, I was visiting an acquaintance who had a small wood yard on the south bank of the Missouri about twenty miles below Fort Buford. He was alone and had no horse to help with the wood cutting. I used my horse to haul his wood to the bank of the river, until one day the horse turned up missing and could not be found on his usual range. This was the third horse I had lost.

I told my companion that if I could find the trail I would follow it as far as it could be followed, no matter where it led. So I armed myself with a blanket, a lariat, some provisions, and the improved Henry rifle that I now carried, which was load enough without impeding my movements, and took the long trail through the woods to the point above. There, not seeing any tracks going up river, I turned about, keeping between the forest and the foothills. When I reached the lower edge of the point I found the familiar hoofprints, showing that the animal was headed down river and going right along as though he had important business.

I suspected at once that someone was astride his back, as the movements of the animal indicated that his rider was hunting game or looking for lost horses. At one place, the signs showed, this fellow stopped to take on meat that he had left hanging in a tree. He was in no hurry and made no effort to conceal his track, and by the moccasin track that appeared at intervals on his trail going in the opposite direction, I gleaned that my man was simply an Indian hunter, who, having made a killing and found a horse, was returning very well satisfied to his camp.

Along in the afternoon, having attained a rise of ground that commanded a view of the next point of timber below, I saw a considerable body of people coming in my direction. Not wishing to be observed until I had satisfied myself as to their friendly character, I remained concealed behind a bush until they had approached nearer, when I saw that the party consisted of a number of families traveling with camp equipage, and on their closer approach I stepped from cover to accost them.

These Indians belonged to the tribes gathered at Fort Berthold, and among them were faces I had seen before. I did not have to question them about my lost horse for I saw him in the crowd, pretty well concealed under a load of skins fastened to a lot of tepee poles that were lashed to the rude Indian saddle that was cinched rather high on his withers.

The procession had halted to converse with me, but I cut short the talk and strode to where the horse was standing and laying hold of the lariat halter that was tied around his jaw, made to unload him. A very stout woman who had hold of the end of the lariat cried out and resisted my efforts, whereupon an elderly Indian who was standing by addressed me in the Dakota language, saying: "Cuda, this horse may belong to you, as you say, but a young man found him in the woods and brought him to our camp. Wait a little, we go a short distance to our stopping place, and the horse will be returned to you."

I replied by making the sign for good (which is a wave of the hand straight out from the heart) and motioned them to proceed. At the camping ground, which was on the bank of the river, an Indian indicated where certain lodges should be erected and the others grouped themselves accordingly. The stout woman unloaded my horse with many exclamations, not at all complimentary to me, I suspect, and removing the lariat, hit the horse on the flank with the end.

Adventures on the Yellowstone

Indian women have a good deal to say about the management in some camps. For instance, they may desire to move camp. Wood may be scarce or too far from camp. The women get together and take down the chief's lodge. The lowering of the chief's lodge is the signal to break camp. Every lodge comes down and is rolled up ready to be packed on horses or sleds.

An Indian caught my horse and a crowd gathered to see the white man make a rope headstall with the lariat I carried. This was a simple affair in the Mexican style, and when adjusted and fitted to the head of my horse proved more humane than the Indian method of putting two half hitches around an animal's lower jaw. Laying the blanket across his back I jumped aboard, which you must know is not an easy thing to do on a loose blanket, and after giving him a drink at the river, sped away on my return journey.

CHAPTER VII

A MILITARY RECONNOISSANCE AND
A WOLF HUNT

A FEW days after the recovery of my horse a
steamboat drew into the bank from down river
and the first man to walk down the gangplank
was that incomparable river man, Captain Grant
Marsh, whose skill as a pilot won him fame in the Civil
War and later on the Yellowstone. He introduced me
to General George A. Forsyth of General Sheridan's
staff, who had at that time a military mission to ascend
the Yellowstone to make some examination of the channel and the country as far as Powder River, also to determine the possibility of steamboat navigation beyond
that point. An adventure of this kind suited me very
well and it was arranged that I should accompany him
on the *Far West,* which Captain Marsh was engaged
to pilot up the Yellowstone. As there was no room on
the boat to carry a horse I decided to leave mine for the
use of my friend at the wood yard. He would find him
useful in his business and the animal would be as safe
there as anywhere.

I embarked, carrying my baggage in one hand, and
was assigned a stateroom, the boat not being crowded
with officers and men until we left Fort Buford. On
reaching that point there ensued a great bustle of preparation on the part of the officers and men detailed for
this much-desired service. The addition of eight officers
and the better part of two companies of infantry with
their equipage and supplies rather crowded the boat and

A Military Reconnoissance

I made shift to find another sleeping place before all the available space had been occupied.

Of the eight officers taken on at Fort Buford not one may now be found on the list of retired officers of the army. They were all fine gentlemen, as one might expect of the regular establishment, and among them I recall Lieutenants Walker and Chance and Major Bryant. There was also, if I am not mistaken, a Captain Ludlow of the engineer corps as a passenger or guest.

The *Far West* entered the mouth of the Yellowstone and steamed slowly against the current. I was curious to see how Captain Marsh would handle the boat through Snaggy Bend, but there was no difficulty, for the river was low and clear, showing plainly all the snags. On the pilot-house platform an officer was engaged in tracing the course of the river. General Forsyth was a close observer of the river banks and the broken country beyond, and he questioned me frequently as to the lay of the land beyond the visible divide and the creeks and valleys that had living streams and springs. Some queries I could not answer positively for the reason that at that period I had never been far from the valley of the Yellowstone, but I pointed out great trails over the low divides made by buffaloes and traveled by Indians.

These trails led to water courses that emptied into the Missouri and continued on north across the upper Missouri to the great grazing grounds of which the Little Rocky and Bear Paw mountains formed the center, and north of these were vast plains where other tribes of Indians and the Red River people obtained hides and meat used in putting up large quantities of pemmican for winter use and trade.

The boat tied to the bank at night, and there I spread

my blanket with instructions to the guard to wake me at one o'clock. Armed with rifle, belted ammunition, knife, and scabbard I made my way through the timber which skirted the river until I reached the edge of the prairie. Then, finding a retired spot, I laid down behind a tree and promptly went to sleep. I rose before daylight, thinking that I was not far enough up the river to make a killing and pack the meat to a bank on the channel where the boat could touch and take it on. The *Far West* would cut loose from her moorings at break of day and the noises of departure on a still morning might alarm the game in the woods and on the edge of the prairie.

It was still dark and I sat down against a cottonwood tree, waiting for the dawn. When it was light enough to see to shoot I began to hunt for antelopes, sure that they would be found on that stretch of prairie confronting me. Yes, there they were, four or five of them, but scattered.

In order to get a shot I must go farther up, but first I must take a long look around to see if there was anything else stirring on the prairie. Everything was quiet, so I picked my way carefully along until I was in position, then fired quickly. I heard the bullet strike his ribs as the antelope bounded, fought to maintain his footing, lunged in a circle, then fell. I could have shot another as they bounded off, but refrained for I was not sure that I could come after him. I turned the slain antelope on his back and with my hunting knife made the usual slit from the brisket to the thigh bone, removed the internal parts, and while the carcass was draining of blood and liquids cut the front feet above the first joint to the bone and inserting them through slits cut between the sinews

"YELLOWSTONE KELLY" ON THE BANK OF THE MISSOURI

STEAMER *FAR WEST* ROUNDING THE BEND

and bones of the hind legs, swung the antelope across one shoulder and started for the bank of the river.

I reached it in about half an hour but found no sign of the *Far West* or of its smoke. I hung the antelope on the limb of a fallen tree in plain sight, also a silk handkerchief that I wore around my neck, and returned to a near point of the prairie where I killed another antelope and got it to the river just as the steamer was rounding the point.

While the boat was picking its way along the channel, bucking the swift current, I looked around and found a lot of dry wood, for whenever the *Far West* stuck her nose into a bank everybody turned out to "wood boat," there being no wood yards on this river and therefore no dry wood except what the beavers and Indians had left.

The *Far West* made a landing near Glendive Creek and the soldiers disembarked and proceeded to unload the bulk of the military supplies and equipage aboard, while General Forsyth and some of the officers ascended a hill near by which commanded a view of the broken country as well as the river line. I accompanied them and pointed out such places as I was familiar with. The cargo, as I remember, was disposed in a way to form some protection in case of attack.

I cannot say how long the boat remained here before it proceeded to the mouth of the Powder River. Perhaps if I had a copy of General Forsyth's report of the trip I should be reminded of some incidents worth recording. I remember that the General was expecting some party traveling overland from the lower country, and that I undertook to spy their approach one clear night from a distant point, but saw nothing but the rough country through which ran an old road made by former expeditions. With the excellent field glasses furnished me I noted buffaloes quietly feeding. Having attained this elevation in the night, I rested in a depression of a ravine that ran to the summit. I remember the faint odors of sage and other herbs that made fragrant the still air as I lay on the ground looking up at the stars, waiting for the dawn.

Having accomplished the object of my trip, it remained for me to make my way back to camp on the river by daylight, as I did not relish remaining in that waterless spot until darkness favored me; so I wormed my way slowly down ravines and gulches, scanning the ground for footprints of Indians and horses, a part of my business for which I needed daylight on ground that was much marked by the footprints of deer and buffaloes. In exposed places where there was no cover I literally crawled from rock to rock or from one shrub to another, such was my caution to avoid the sharp eyes of some prowling Indian, for I knew that they thought nothing of lying concealed all day without water when on the lookout for some enemy, or in a willow-covered eagle trap on a high point motionless for hours waiting for the great bird to drop for its bait, when it is seized by the legs with eager clutch and deprived of the prized tail feathers.

At Fort Buford I shook hands with General Forsyth, and so ended the trip up the Yellowstone. A very pleasant gentleman, quiet and reserved, not much given to recounting past deeds and events, never a word of Beecher Island or the stiff fight and defense made there.[1]

---

[1] General Forsyth has himself told the story of his remarkable Beecher Island fight in September, 1868, in his book, *The Soldier* (New York, 1900), Vol. II.—ED.

A Military Reconnoissance

Before long I began to feel the need of change again. Late in the year (1873), one of Broadwater's bull trains rolled along on its way to Helena, and the leader wanted a man familiar with the country to show him the route through the Indian country. I was the man. I joined the train while it was strung out on the road between Fort Peck and Milk River. Skirting the edge of the Little Rockies, never out of sight of buffaloes, we finally reached an icy plain along which were many bands of buffaloes. We made a camp on this plain, which commanded a view of a large extent of country along the Missouri and beyond it as far south as a group of mountains bordering Judith River.

There were buffaloes feeding within half a mile and I took my rifle and started afoot to get some meat. I approached to within seventy-five yards of a bunch of cows that stood unafraid gazing at me. There was some choice of meat here, for there were many two- or three-year-old heifers and young bulls. Though it seemed doubtful that they would stay for nearer approach I walked along for ten or fifteen yards, for I was mindful that I carried a .44 Henry and the little flat-nosed bullet did not always stop a bull at seventy-five yards. Selecting a two-year-old heifer I let drive and she did not go many yards before falling inert on the ground. The herd, of course, at the shot fled to some distance. Evidently these buffaloes had not been disturbed for some time. I packed some of the choice parts back to camp and returned with my saddle horse for the rest of the meat and the fine skin of dark silky fur, for I judged it would make a fine robe when dressed and properly smoked.

Meanwhile, a couple of strangers rode into camp and made themselves known as Bill Norris and another (whose name I no longer recall) from the little post of Carroll on the right bank of the Missouri. Norris appraised the fat meat that I unloaded by saying, "When I see fat meat like that I am sure going to camp with it." At my invitation they helped themselves to some of the ribs, which they proceeded to roast at the cook's fire with a zest that made me suspect they hadn't tasted buffalo meat for some time. Perhaps they needed an appetizer in that biting air, for presently everybody was roasting ribs, to the discomfort of the cook, who could not get near his fire.

Our foreman, or wagon master, was a very decent fellow, as were all of these Montana men, especially the cook, a big, bearded fellow whose gruff call of "grub pile" brought everyone pronto to where an iron kettle of coffee and Dutch ovens of frying meats and hot biscuits awaited attention. The cook had choice names for some of his concoctions, not listed in any menu save the unwritten one of a bull train.

In a few days we reached a point where the old wagon road wound around toward the west end of the Bear Paw Mountains and connected with the roads and trails of the north country that converge to Fort Benton on the upper Missouri River. Here I left this Montana outfit and turned aside to make the crossing of the river above Carroll.

Carroll was situated on the right bank of the Missouri in a narrow strip of cottonwood timber, the bank being only about four or five feet above high water. The channel was close to this bank, which made it convenient for steamers to close haul and tie to a tree. There was a trade store, storehouse, and factor's residence, also a few shacks and cabins. I don't remember seeing any Indians there except a war party that came down the breaks, fired a few shots, and retired with greater speed, their hurry being hastened by an unorganized body of hunters and sojourners who followed them thirty miles.

In a small way Carroll was a rendezvous for hunters and trappers, who outfitted there, the region on both sides being stocked with game of all sorts, including fur-bearing animals. The factor, doing business for the firm of Ashby of Helena, was a pleasant gentleman and was kind enough to lend me one or two volumes of the prose works of Edgar Allen Poe. I also met here some old acquaintances. One was Jim Cooper, an excellent type of the men who come out from the state of Georgia, well read, a good talker, and fine fellow generally. Then there was Blount, of a different type, hailing from the Carolinas, honest and reliable. I seem to hear his soft southern accent, telling of the time the Indians had them coralled in a small stockade. A negro stood undecided with an axe in his hand: "What shall I do, Blount?" "Frow down that axe, you black bugger, and go to fouting." Some of these Southerners were called "galvanized yanks." Having been taken prisoners during the war, they were released on taking an oath not to take up arms against the Union cause, and drifted to the mining regions and plains of the Far West.

Here I again met "Red Mike" Welsh, who gave me shelter after my first encounter with hostile Sioux. He was a cool man with a rifle and a very good shot. I recall one occasion when we were about to start from Fort Buford for Fort Peck, a white man of our acquaintance came and asked to travel with us for protection. He was a man of good character and I think had been in the military service. He had espoused an excellent woman of Indian blood, and by her had two or more young children. They had for conveyance a Red River cart, drawn by a pony that belonged to a young man, a relative perhaps, who also accompanied them.

About the second camp the Indian became dissatisfied for some reason and in the morning while we were packing to break camp saddled the cart pony and started off at a swift gallop up the river. Mike was the only one in the party who had his horse saddled, and before anything was said, after the first outcry of the woman, he had mounted and was in quick pursuit. He very soon overhauled the Indian, who jumped from his steed and disappeared into the woods, and we shortly proceeded as before.

With four other men I organized a little hunt, from which we returned with a quantity of skins, among them a very large elk skin, bagged by a certain member of the coterie, who, when skinning an elk, took great delight in leaving as much meat on the hide as possible. The trader knew a bit about skins and when all were weighed and paid for he left the elk skin on the scales, and I used to go in there every few days to see how much the skin had lightened. I will venture to say that there were over ten pounds of meat on that hide that did not belong there, and was only fit for fertilizer. Indians never resort to such practices as this. The skins they bring to the trader are clean, dry, well stretched, and neatly packed, as if prepared for their own use.

I had not at this time met Sandy Morris, whom I shall have occasion later to mention, but I ran across Bill Atwood, one of whose adventures in the early seventies I still recall. With one companion he was hunting and trapping along the upper Missouri. They had agreed that if they should be surprised by Indians each would grab whatever was at hand and strike for shelter. One day while in camp they were suddenly fired into by a roving war party and each grabbed something and started for some near-by trees. After the Indians had been put to flight the two men compared notes: "Well," said Atwood, "I brought a loaf of bread but I see an Indian has shot a hole through the center of it." "Let's see," said Jack. Thereupon the sack was up-ended and out rolled the camp grindstone.

Once when a war party of Sioux made a raid on Carroll, from which they beat a hasty retreat, one of the men and I raced to the hills to see what we could find and there ran into a beautiful black mare tied to a tree. My companion was first to put his hand on her and so claimed the find. We left her tied while we concealed ourselves near by, thinking that the owner might return for his property, but he failed to appear. The mare proved a swift runner in the trial races around Carroll, and I afterwards purchased her.

When in July, 1876, the columns returned to the Yellowstone from pursuit of the hostiles and the expedition was about to break up, I happened along, having come over the divide from Judith Basin on hearing the news of General Custer's last stand. Several infantry units were camped along the river, some about to march to their stations in Montana, others waiting for transportation eastward. I sold the mare and her handsome black colt to an officer commanding one of the companies, Captain Cusick, whom I had met several years earlier when he was stationed at Fort Buford. The soldiers of the company straightway made a pet of the colt, whose well-being and comfort was assured from that moment.

Along in the winter of 1874 I noticed a red-headed, freckle-faced man going about Carroll with his arm in a sling. He proved to be Sandy Morris. We soon became acquainted and I learned his story. He and George Horn had rigged out and gone to the foot of Bear Paw Mountains, that debatable ground claimed alike by the Crows, Blackfeet, and Sioux, then the winter range of herds of buffaloes that came down from their summer range on the northern plains to find shelter and grass in its lee. The particular purpose of the hunters was to string out a lot of buffalo baits for the wolves that hang closely to the herds of buffaloes, hamstringing the cows and bulls and worrying the young calves in the spring. They carried a supply of strychnine to poison the baits. They had a saddle horse apiece, and one pack horse. They put out several baits in favorable situations and were in a fair way to secure a good lot of skins, as the wolves appeared to be plentiful. Camp was made one day in an exposed place at the head of Cow Creek, where there was a lone cottonwood tree. After a light fall of snow they went along the base of the mountain for a mile and killed a bull, which they poisoned. Returning to camp just before dusk, they built a fire against a big log about forty feet from the tree and after they had had their supper sat in front of the fire with their backs to it. In this situation a war party of Santee Sioux, who had watched their movements, approached their camp after dark, and having secured their horses, fired a volley into them from behind this tree.

The two men, though hit by this fusillade, jumped to

their feet and returned the fire. Horn fired one shot and then fell prone, while Sandy emptied his Winchester in the direction of the redskins, who, thinking they had overshot or missed the white men, retired precipitately. George Horn was shot through the chest and Sandy was shot with slugs in the shoulder and neck. Sandy, ignoring the danger, carried his partner, who complained of being cold, to the fire and made him comfortable with blankets and robes, but he expired after a few minutes. Covering the dead man with blankets and canvas, Sandy struck out into the night and snow and next morning reached a cabin on the Missouri occupied by two white men. They brought him into Carroll, where a party was organized at once and went after the body of Horn.

In a few weeks Sandy had recovered from his wounds and one day he offered me a half interest in the enterprise if I would furnish a pack horse and go with him to the Bear Paw Mountains and help secure and skin the wolves that had probably accumulated around the baits. I questioned him about the lay of the land around them, the water courses and camping grounds, and in a few days we had made our arrangements, obtained needed supplies from the trading store, and were ready to march. I had provided a good stout pack animal and this was the only horse we took.

It was pleasant going along the bottom lands of the river with an occasional divergence where the river channel had eroded the low bluffs. Going up one sharp ridge, the pack horse slipped and rolled end over end to the bottom. I thought every minute he would break his neck, but he came up standing, with nothing worse than a good shaking. With the pack it was different, however, and we had to take it off and rearrange the load.

When we arrived at the mouth of Cow Creek we stopped for supper, after which we packed again and proceeded along well-worn trails that cut the dry channel of the creek many times in the first few miles. The cabin of the two white men who had assisted Morris stood on the bank of the Missouri some distance below the mouth of Cow Creek, and was abandoned.

Just ahead of us on the trail was a band of buffaloes numbering a hundred or more. They would scarcely get out of our way. We would drive our pack horse before us until he was within a few yards of them, when they would make a spurt for a short distance, and we would repeat the maneuver. After dark the shadowy outline of a war house loomed before us on one side of the trail and we halted, intending to camp for the night.

War houses in that region were built according to the material at hand. If slabs and poles were available the structure was made in the shape of a conical tepee, thick enough for shelter and protection, with the open entrance overlapping and the loose top affording an exit for smoke. A similar shelter was sometimes built in the shape of an unfinished Mandan wigwam. The one we had come upon was conical and shapely, and showed signs of having been occupied recently by Indians.

Our nag was turned loose to pick up what he could, while we made ourselves as comfortable in the war house as we could without a fire. A couple of matches showed us where best to arrange our blankets and we were soon settled for a good night's rest. It may be thought that we would have been safer by turning off to one side of the gulch and concealing ourselves in a ravine, but it was all rough rocks, snow, and frozen, uneven ground and we preferred the comfort of a dry habitation and were not intimidated by the knowledge that this war house had been built by a roving party of Indians who might again seek its shelter at any time. By dawn we were out after the horse and by daylight were on the trail, as there was no water to make coffee and to melt snow was too slow for our business.

As we neared the head of Cow Creek I shot a black-tail buck and poisoned the carcass. Throwing the bloody hide over the pack, we had proceeded only a short distance when we ran into a herd of bulls. I had never seen so many together in the late winter time. They stared for a moment, intently if not fiercely, then as if at word of command up went their tails and instantly they were trotting in a close body directly toward us. I shouted to Sandy: "They are going to charge us, throw your overcoat over the pack!" He was just in time and the bulls, no longer seeing red, turned to one side. I do not know what might have happened if the hide had not been promptly covered. The spectacle of being surrounded and charged by a lot of bulls would have been more than comical.

When we reached the spot where Sandy and his partner had been fired upon, I saw the cottonwood tree and the log and ashes of their fire near it. We did not find the wolves as plentiful as Sandy had expected, but in a few days we secured enough to make a load. After we had put out a few more baits we cached some of our things and returned without further adventure to Carroll.

After resting a week at Carroll, during which the wolves along the Bear Paw were being afforded an opportunity to become familiar with the choice meats prepared for their palates and to overcome their inherent distrust of food not killed by their kind, we made a new start for the head of Cow Creek, and in better trim, for a saddle horse was added to our equipment, to ride or pack as desired.

On entering the gulch of Cow Creek we camped in the same war house we had utilized on our first excursion. Some traveling Indians had left strips of fat buffalo meat hanging to a crosspole above the center, which we proceeded to consume. Evidently they intended to return the same way. Their tracks were plain in the morning and only a day or two old. When Sandy saw the moccasin prints he remarked: "Our trails are likely to meet if this thing keeps on." "Yes," I replied, "and if they leave some more fat meat we will be more chary of making use of it."

We made camp on the spot where Sandy and George Horn had been attacked, and from there went along the base of the mountain, where most of our baits were. No Indians were seen until we had skinned all but two or three of our last pile of wolves. Then a rifle shot sounded a little way off along the edge of the mountain and we debated whether to quit at once or finish skinning, as it looked stormy. Soon we saw some Indians traveling parallel to our course. As we were in plain sight they evidently saw us, therefore we were not much concerned. Presently three of the men detached themselves from the main party and came toward us and we waited their approach. They proved to be "Stonies" from across the Canadian border, who had come out with their women on a hunting expedition. They were as black as burnt wood, the result of camping in the mountains and using pine for fuel. I could not talk to them to any advantage as they were as poor in the sign language as I was.

We were now through with the Bear Paw Mountains, and returning to camp for our equipage we laid our course across country for the Missouri, camping for the night in the cedar breaks. Crossing the river on the ice (it was now about February, 1875) we made camp just above the river, intending to remain a few days and see what could be added to our load in the way of pelts.

I went out early in the morning to look at the country and put out a bait. Sandy had some traps to look after. The river passed between high banks here and the trail along the cut bank was narrow and icy. Ten feet down was the snow-covered solid ice. Right there I came upon the scene of a tragedy. Blood, hair, gnawed bones, and the trampled surface of the ice told of a buck pursued and surrounded by wolves. Here, according to the story told in the snow, he made his stand, panting and distressed, while the wolves leaped upon him *en masse*.

Picking my way carefully along the treacherous trail, I came suddenly upon a blind pocket on my left in which was an old bull lying down. I could not turn around or run without the risk of slipping and falling to the ice below. When I spied the animal he was about thirty feet away, but he proved to be a very lively bull, for he sprang to his feet instantly and with head down and tail up came for me. I shoot from the left shoulder, but there was no time for that operation, so, quickly shifting my little Henry rifle, I held it on that grisly ornament of his face, the forelock, heavy with sand and matted with burrs, which hung between his eyes, and when he was about ten feet away let him have it. He dropped on the instant.

"Yellowstone Kelly"

I felt immensely relieved, for you cannot always count on a successful issue in shooting at the forehead of a buffalo bull. I stood by and contemplated my unsought and unlovely prize, lying prone on the frozen ground. He was too tough to skin for a bait, for your wolf is a discriminating animal unless starved. The hide and fur showed signs of being close to the off-season, though it had the familiar look of some of the stiff and heavy skins that the contractor used to work up into winter overcoats for Uncle Sam's soldiers serving in below-zero climates. Neither the tongue nor the marrow bones appealed to me, so I went my way until I found a suitable place for one or two baits.

Sandy was amused at my recital of the encounter with the bull and was curious to see the kind of trap I was caught in, so the next morning we went out of our way a quarter of a mile to look at the place. Tying our horses to a shrub, we walked down into the pocket, the only outlet being toward the river bank where I had stood. Looking around, Sandy speculated over the vagaries of chance by which an undertaking might fail through a simple accident. I remarked that worse things might happen. We led our horses into the low cedars and I shot two antelopes where I had thought to find deer.

The carcasses lay about sixty or seventy yards apart and our horses were between. Sandy started to cut up the farther one while I proceeded to the other and was about to engage it with my sheath knife when by merest chance I looked around and saw some objects in motion about one hundred yards away that struck me as very odd. They came over a little ridge in single file and looked like young cows. While I was observing them under the brim of my hat they went out of sight into a hol-

KELLY AND SANDY MORRIS MEET A YANKTON WAR PARTY

low. I signaled Sandy and we started for our horses, but before we got to them the cows had transformed themselves into a party of Indians, habited in buffalo robes, who were coming boldly in our direction.

Being ready for them, I held up my hand and signaled them to halt. They complied and the leader put his robe on the ground, placed on it his gun, bow and quiver of arrows, knife and sheath, then strode toward us. I said to Sandy: "Keep your eyes on the crowd and if they edge up closer warn them back." "You bet I will," he answered. He was a little excited and nervous, but true blue.

The leader was now before us, an unprepossessing-looking fellow with remnants of red and yellow paint on his face. He demanded tobacco. I asked Sandy to give him a piece, and he reached down into his pocket and extracted two pieces of plug, one large piece and one smaller. He held out the smaller piece, but the Indian made no motion to take it.

"I want both pieces, I want it all!" he said. Without a word Sandy shoved both pieces into his pocket and quickly raising his rifle, shouted to those behind to keep back. I warned the Indian to keep his men back. "That man will shoot," I said.

"Do you want to fight?" he demanded. "No," I replied, "not for a piece of tobacco."

He then expressed his willingness to take the piece offered, but I said: "No, go back to your party and travel around." I made a sweeping gesture with my hand at the last word, adding, "too much talk," and cocking my gun motioned him to depart. He went quickly without a word, mad all through. Stopping a moment to harangue his party, he took the lead, and describing a circle to the left, passed over the hill. When we saw them again they were half a mile away and still going to the north. It was fortunate that I saw them when I did, for I am satisfied that if they could have got close enough unobserved they would have poured a volley into us and counted some coup.

I heard of them afterward; it seems that the Pole Cat's son, Yanktonai, from the Porcupine, north of Milk River, formed a war party to steal horses from the mountain Crows. They had a skirmish with a party of Crows and got away with one or two wounded.

Sandy and I returned to camp without delay, for the neighborhood had lost its charm for us that trip. Not that we were afraid of this party, now that they had been discovered, but we were concerned for the safety of our horses. If we lost them there would be extraordinary toil and hardship expended in an effort to recover them. Better to get out easy and come again when we were ready.

When everything was packed and ready for the trail, Sandy asked: "What about the traps?" Sure enough, we had forgotten them. We took the packs off, and mounting, rode up the river and recovered the traps. That night we camped in the cottonwoods, a great relief after the wind-swept barren ridges of Cow Creek and the foot of the Bear Paw Mountains.

CHAPTER VIII

HUNTING IN THE JUDITH BASIN

THE summer of 1875 I spent mostly in cruising in and about the Judith Basin and vicinity. The basin proper was too open and exposed to afford good hunting, but southeast of Judith Mountain on the slopes and cedar ridges extending to the Musselshell River and beyond to the breaks of the Yellowstone was a veritable hunters' paradise for game of all kinds, including elk, deer, and mountain sheep, and cinnamon, black, and brown bear. I noted also that it was a good country to run into war parties of the Sioux, Crow, and Blackfeet tribes.

In the basin Major Reed and his partner, Bowles, had erected a cabin for trade, and this was the gathering place for hunters, trappers, explorers, and Indians, for there was a highway, or at least a wagon trail, leading in directly to Bozeman and the mining camps that dotted the valleys and gulches of Montana. Did I make the acquaintance of George Bird Grinnell about this time or was it the following spring, near Reed's ranch? I cannot remember, but it was only for a moment and he was off with his guide. In that lonely region, teeming with game and exuberance of mountain flora, he had no time to spare. But fresh in memory is the Major and his log cabin set in grass land beside a clear stream and close by the funeral lodge of Long Horse, a noted Crow chief, who was killed at the head of his warriors while charging the hostile Sioux concealed in thick bush and timber.

"Yellowstone Kelly"

Back again in Carroll in the early fall of this year, arrangements were made to exploit the region southeast of the Judith Range for wolves, and a party of four, the Erwin brothers, Mike Welsh, and myself, formed an association for that purpose. The Erwins had a team and wagon, while Mike and I had a saddle horse apiece, besides a pack horse which I furnished. We proposed to go in style and comfort. Among our effects were two cast-iron Dutch ovens, a small grindstone, shovel and pick, two axes, half a pound of strychnine, and provisions and ammunition to last until spring. All this cost a pretty sum of money, but the trader had faith that we would make good in the spring with furs and skins, for of course we had some traps as well as poison.

We made our camp in the Cone Butte Pass, near its outlet to the south, where there were some deep crevices in the rim-rock in which we could cache our skins as they accumulated. We designed to build a cabin as a base from which to visit our baits for wolves, which would be scattered over a circuit of fifty miles or more if hostile war parties did not interfere too much with our movements.

We remained at the Cone Butte to hunt while the ground was new and undisturbed. While the deer and elk were in good condition we wanted to put up several hundred pounds of fat meat by the use of salt which we had brought along for this purpose. Later on, all game would deteriorate in flesh and become poor. Primarily the buffalo wolf and the timber wolf were the lure that induced us to pitch our tents in this isolated region that lay so conveniently between the Sioux and Crows, and we did not want to kill any game animals other than what were needed for baits for wolves and food for ourselves. The slope of the Judith was ideal for deer and elk. One man stayed in camp. The other two might choose to hunt together, but I delighted to hunt alone, to wander through the open timber and grassy openings, not caring whether I saw a deer or not until it came time to return to camp. Then I got busy, for I could not go back empty-handed.

One morning I had not gone far when I struck a deer trail and presently came to where the print of a bear's track came into it. I followed along with gun held in both hands ready for action. Soon another track appeared, all very fresh, and they might have been black bears for I noted several flat rocks and rotten logs that had been turned over in a search for bugs and mice. I walked very slowly along the trail, expecting to stumble on to one any moment. I was now in the pines with low bushes and rocks scattered around. About two hundred yards farther on two more bears, making large tracks, joined the procession, making four bears on the trail somewhere just ahead of me. The trail was now beaten smooth, obliterating all deer tracks.

I stopped to meditate on the situation. My curiosity was aroused, for I wanted to see what this drift of bears toward one little deer trail led to. It might be there was a carcass of deer or elk ahead, which the keen scent of bruin had detected. If I kept on I would be obliged to kill a bear or two, if they did not kill me; the skin would be of little value, and heavy as lead to pack. Bear meat, unless it is very young and fat, like a sucking pig, is not good eating. So I hesitated, being alone, but finally decided to go ahead a little way to where an opening led higher up the ridge to the deer thickets.

Before I reached the point where I intended to turn

off I heard two shots in quick succession ahead and to the right, followed by the whine of a she-bear. I quickened my footsteps in the direction of the firing, feeling certain that one of my companions had run into the snarl of bears and was having a picnic all by himself.

The shots, of course, stirred game in the vicinity, and watching my opportunity I brought down a young buck. Noting a fallen pine near where he fell, I pressed on and discovered Mike in the act of skinning a good-sized cinnamon. Hearing my shot, he had suspected who it was and resumed his job of removing the hide. "I first saw two black bears," he said; "while watching their antics the cinnamon came within shooting distance, and paying no further attention to the black bears, I let him have it. He started for me and I plugged him again, and he laid down to rest." The cinnamon had good hair and I suggested that he hang it up and we would come after it and the other meat with our saddle horses. This was agreed to, and after hanging the skin on the limb of a tree and flagging it we separated. I returned to dress the buck I had killed, after which I went higher up the ridge and killed another.

The main cabin of green logs was to have a stone fireplace in one corner and everything fixed comfortable as a place of retreat and rest during the stormy weather, for it was our intention at the approach of cold weather to cache the greater part of our supplies and accumulated skins in some dry and secret place safe from the inquisitive eyes of prowling natives and depart with saddle and pack horses to some buffalo grounds near the big bend of the Musselshell.

The carcass of a buffalo loaded with three-eighths of an ounce of crystallized strychnine and frozen to resist

Hunting in the Judith Basin

the angry onslaught of a pack of wolves was no mean
aid to swell the hunter's collection of pelts. From ten to
fifty large wolves are sometimes found stretched in all
kinds of postures around the bait and if the hunter does
not visit his baits every two or three days, he will find an
occasional eagle, raven, or magpie dead or disabled.
These scavengers of the air tear holes in the bellies of
half frozen wolves (the belly being the last part to
freeze) and extract the swallowed poisoned meat,
which, if they get enough of it, places them *hors de combat*. For this reason frozen wolves were usually put in
a pile and covered with brush or snow until a chinook
wind or spring weather afforded opportunity to thaw
them sufficiently to be skinned. Sometimes a salable
hide is manufactured from the mutilated skins of two
wolves by clever matching and patching.

One evening while we were at the camp in Cone Butte
Pass a party of eight or ten Crow Indians suddenly
made their appearance while we were eating. They were
afoot for a wonder, and came in that noiseless way ha-
bitual to the moccasin wearer. They were friendly, and
when we accosted them they cried out "Absaroke! Bot-
sots!" which means Crows, or good friends. After shaking hands all around, the circle about the fire was extended and our visitors were given a cup of coffee each
with bread and meat. On first acquaintance Indians do
not have much to say until they have broken their fast
and smoked the pipe.

They are very observant of everything about them,
though without appearing to be so. As a rule the wild
Indians of the mountains and plains are well-bred in
company, and possess a natural politeness and decorum
of manner well worth observing. Transport one of them

suddenly to a crowded drawing-room, and though the change would be startling it is safe to say that he would rise to the occasion and in bearing, at least, would conduct himself with all the ease and nonchalance of a man of the world. Of course Indians differ as other peoples do, and there was a marked difference in the scale of intelligence, in early days, before the government established schools among them. The Crows differ from the Sioux in feature and dress, and very much in language. Within the border of Wyoming and Montana territories there were eight or more tribes of Indians, each with a language of its own, differing from the others as much as English differs from Russian. Of these the Sioux, of which there are several dialects, is perhaps the most musical, affording a copious flow of words.

The men of the Crow tribe dress their hair in two long braids, wrapped in strips of otter skin which hang on either side of the head in front halfway to the waist. Over the forehead and banged with an upward curve the hair is stiffened and kept in place by an application of white clay. Around the neck brass ornaments and pink shells are hung. Leggings and blankets, or buffalo robes, plain or garnished with bead work or painted characters, complete the costume, while fringed or feathered leather cases for gun or bow add to the picturesqueness of their attire.

Our visitors disposed of their food in silence. Then an old fellow who was treated with some deference brought to light a long buckskin sack, from the depths of which he drew a redstone pipe, then a long, flat wooden stem with a bit of feather, which he proceeded with great deliberation to fit into the pipe. A request was then made for tobacco, and a piece of plug being produced it was given to another Indian, who proceeded to cut it up fine in the hollow of his hand and mix it with a proper quantity of larb as described on an earlier page. With the larb the Crows have a fancy for mixing a minute pinch of the dried castors of the beaver.

The tobacco prepared and the pipe filled and lighted, the old fellow takes a few whiffs, then touches the bowl of the pipe to the ground, after which it is held aloft for a moment while he follows it with his inscrutable gaze. Then the stem is pointed first to the east, then to the west, and after a few puffs to keep alive the medicine it is passed to the right around the circle, each one taking a couple of whiffs and passing it to his neighbor. This is the ceremony, somewhat curtailed, of passing round the pipe. The office of pipe bearer approaches that of standard bearer and is usually held by the chief haranguer or wizard of the party. Conversation was now in order, and the leader of the Crows asked where the rest of our party was. On being told that all were present and accounted for he expressed surprise by placing his hand over his mouth.

"Friend," he said, "the Sioux village is only two sleeps away and their war parties pass very close to this mountain; whatever can induce you to stay here?"

The answer to this was that we were hunters, that we carried medicine for wolves and in our guns carried medicine for war parties, if they interfered with us; that our hearts were "good," but that we were very bad people to trifle with. This sort of talk met their understanding and was assented to without comment. The old fellow told us his village was only half a day's journey from our camp, and while running buffaloes the day before they had heard our shots and curiosity had led them to investigate. All but two of the party were young men.

As the day wore on they threw off their natural reserve and joked and laughed like boys. The young men sang a hymn or chant of friendship in low tones to a wild but not unpleasing air. The leader said they were glad to get away from camp, for the women and old men had been wailing all summer over the loss of twenty-two warriors who had perished in battle with the Sioux. From the story it appeared that in the previous autumn twenty-three Crows had started on a horse-stealing raid against the Sioux on the Yellowstone. They discovered two large camps of the enemy in the bad lands before reaching the Yellowstone, and succeeded in rounding up and driving off, unperceived, a number of horses. They traveled along until dark, then camped to rest for the night. One of the party, however, refused to stop, and taking his share of the horses kept on his way. He did not propose to take chances so near the enemy. He was the only one who came out alive.

The Sioux discovered their presence and pursued them. They came in sight of the Crows at daylight. Being surrounded and outnumbered ten to one, they managed to gain the crest of a hill, where they constructed a rude breastwork of rocks and defended themselves with the bravery of despair as long as their ammunition lasted. The Sioux harassed them with fire from every rock, bush, and hollow in the vicinity, and when the Crows were reduced to five or six in number a charge was made by the young and untrained warriors of the camp, to whom was presented a grand opportunity of winning the aboriginal spurs and counting a first coup under the eyes and encouragement of their own people.

Hunting in the Judith Basin

Several of the Sioux bit the dust in this encounter before the Crows were exterminated. One of the Crows who feigned death turned on his side and sent an arrow halfway through a young brave as he was riding full tilt over him. Not satisfied with this he sprang up and pulled the Indian off his horse and had actually mounted the animal when he was shot down. Their people, meanwhile, in the far Crow camps near the upper Missouri River, knew nothing of this great disaster and for days after the return of the one man a lookout was kept for the rest of the party, but they failed, of course, to materialize. Finally, their fate was learned in a roundabout way from the whites, who received the news by mail from one of the agencies for the Sioux on the lower river.

The conversation was carried on partly in the Sioux language and partly by the aid of signs, it having transpired early in the interview that as a medium for the exchange of ideas and sentiments we struck no common ground in the Crow tongue. The Sioux tongue is pretty well understood by the Indians of the northern plains, and the sign language adapts itself as gracefully and as readily to these Indians as their robes and blankets.

By the middle of November we were ready to strike out for other hunting grounds, and after caching most of our belongings we gathered our saddles and pack ponies together, left the log cabin in the Cone Butte Pass, and turned our faces southeast toward the Musselshell. No one in the party was familiar with this part of the country, beyond such knowledge as was gained from observation from mountain tops or gleaned from other hunters of the Crows.

Avoiding the trails along the creeks, we traveled

along the cedar ridges. Droves of black-tail deer on either side turned off down the ravines or scattered among the cedars. Buffaloes would look at us for a moment and then trot down the slope out of sight. Late in the afternoon we came upon a substantial war house and concluded to camp for the night. This war house was well put up, roomy and comfortable, and had probably held twenty-five of the red rascals who constructed it. Our packs were transferred to the interior and the stock was turned loose, for there was abundant grass near at hand.

As there was some daylight left yet, we set out in different directions to look at the country and see what the prospect was for fur and skins. At night we gathered around our little fire, drank coffee or tea and ate fat venison or buffalo meat, with which we made it a point to keep well supplied. Flour we had, and one of the party took pride in making light, sweet bread, baked in a frying pan, braced on edge in front of the fire. Smoking and conversation usually filled the evening.

After looking around it was agreed that the country promised well for our business and we decided to remain for a few days and put out some baits in the neighborhood. The howling of the wolves at night was almost incessant. One would start a prolonged howl, then another would take it up in a different key; others would join in quick succession, producing a medley of most satisfying discord; but for a mournful howl, commend me to an old dog-wolf in a storm; the hoarse notes swell and die away with each succeeding blast like a veritable demon of the gale.

Timber wolves have yellowish markings on the side. The buffalo wolves we found north of the Missouri were coarse haired compared with the gray wolves obtained near Flat Willow Creek; some were pure white, others different shades of cream, the full-grown ones being of the very largest size. Man has nothing to fear on the score of wolves in this region; as for the wretched little coyotes that were ki-hi-ing all hours of the night and sometimes in daylight, we considered them hardly worth skinning. It is true that the hair and fur is of finer texture than that of the gray wolf and is better adapted to some uses. Commercially they were of little value to us, and they devoured valuable baits placed by members of our party, at some labor, to attract bigger game.

We put out only three buffalo baits at this camp, the weather not being cold enough for our purpose, but we tacked down about twenty large wolf-skins, intending to take them up on our return from down country. I do not remember clearly just what course we pursued to reach Flat Willow Creek, whether we cut across the cedar ridges or traveled farther down the country before turning aside, but I know that we camped in the open and slaughtered a lot of deer in the cedar ridges opposite. The creek bed was dry or nearly so, and snow was melted for camp use. We reasoned that no large war party bent on a big enterprise would attack us, for there was little to gain and much to lose.

We found a retired place in a coulee to store our skins, and traveled down stream to where the Flat Willow was joined by creeks coming in from the east. Here a war house was found and camp made for a day, when the elder Erwin and Mike Welch left us with packs bound for the rough country to the east, to place baits. Jean Erwin and I remained at this camp several days.

One afternoon I went afoot across the hills to put out

a bait. Keeping well in the hollows, I had not traveled more than a mile when I perceived a buffalo cow lying down in a prairie dog village. "Now," I said to myself after looking all around, "if I can kill that cow right where she is in the prairie dog village, it will be in an excellent situation for wolves." It was an exposed place and it took me some time to work along the depressions in order to gain a point of vantage without disturbing the cow. I did not want to shoot hastily and have the animal run off to some hollow to die, for although I was an indifferent marksman, I always liked to kill my game with as little pain as possible to the quarry.

Suddenly two large wolves came into view and trotted up to the cow, which got up at once, facing them with lowered head, and I then saw that she was lame. The wolves acted with superb indifference and even turned their backs to her, then they trotted down toward me and came to within fifteen yards of where I was crouched, motionless and observant. After observing me casually for a moment, they returned to the cow as they had come. I could not fail to note the abandoned grace of action in these wild animals, every movement exact and businesslike, as though time were a factor to be considered. As soon as they left me I took the opportunity to creep up closer, and as the cow turned with lowered head to repel the wolves, now about to attack, I placed a shot back of the shoulder and she fell without a struggle. The wolves made off at the shot.

When I approached the carcass of the cow to prepare it for wolf bait I saw about a hundred yards away, some standing, some sitting on their haunches, twenty or more large wolves. They formed a very pretty picture on the yellow and gray prairie, that was partly wind-

swept of snow. What surprised me was their utter un-
concern when I came into view. They were lined up in
a row as though they had been bidden to a feast and
were not particular as to how it was served.

Laying my gun and belt on the ground, I tackled the
carcass of the buffalo cow and soon had it prepared with
strychnine in the manner that I have elsewhere described. My audience of wolves took an unusual interest
in the work and scarcely moved during its continuance.
I surmised that this was not the first time they had posed
as spectators of a meat-carving entertainment, and that
they may have followed Indians on a buffalo hunt.
Though uninvited guests, I would not allow their appre-
ciation to pass unrewarded.

When I had finished I washed the blood off my knife
and hands in a bank of snow, threw away the empty
vials that had held the poison, and backed off leisurely
toward the hollow by which my approach had been
made, whence I took my way to the war house.

Close to the war house there was a large beaver dam
with evidence of recent occupation. In our leisure mo-
ments we tried our hands at digging out the underground lodgers, an easy feat, seemingly, as there was no
water running in the creek bed and the pond created by
the dam, though fed by the spring, was frozen solid. We
had to give it up, however, for the light prospecting
pick and superannuated shovel in our possession made
little impression on the outworks and we concluded that
beavers were friendly creatures and good neighbors.

In building this dam the clever animals had chosen a
season when the creek was at a low stage of water, had
chiseled a cottonwood tree near the bank so that it fell at
a sharp angle up stream, and had repeated the operation

on the other bank, so that the head of one tree rested on and interlocked with the other. This mass and weight of green top had caused the stream to rise and the added weight of water to straighten out the trees, in the process of which a rigid interlocking of branches resulted. It was then that the beavers got busy with brush, stakes, mud, and tails to anchor the whole mass superimposed upon the clay and gravelly bottom. Thus a foundation was made to harbor one or more families of these intelligent and useful rodents. Useful, because they hold the waters back in a too rapidly draining country, thereby causing savannas to form, with resulting vegetation for their own subsistence and that of other creatures, including man. As one of our party remarked, "the beaver is the water farmer of the plains."

At night a small fire dimly lighted the interior of the war house. The frying pans and tins had been put to one side and the slender sacks of flour, sugar, and coffee reposed in their respective places in a parfleche container hanging to a cross-piece to keep it out of the way of mice. My companion and I sat on opposite sides of the lodge engaged in making willow pegs for stretching wolf-skins, wondering, meanwhile, where our partners were at that moment.

On the third morning Jean Erwin and I made the round of our baits and piled up many wolves. At the place where I had had an attentive audience while cutting up the body of the cow, we found twenty-two large wolves around the bait, though some had got several hundred yards away before succumbing to the effects of the powerful poison. From the wolfer's point of view they were beauties. Two were almost pure white, one was of a creamy color, and several had the tawny markings of the timber wolf; the rest were gray, but of finer hair than the buffalo wolf. They were frozen too hard to skin, so we piled them in a near-by coulee and covered them with snow in a spot out of range of the sun's rays.

The country round about for a distance of three or four miles was now pretty well marked with our shoe and pony prints and we concluded to move camp. Our skins and pelts were well secreted and those we had pegged to the ground would not suffer if left in that state until our return.

We traveled down the creek and camped on another tributary. Scarcely had we completed the task of putting out two or three baits when a two-day blizzard set in that confined us closely to an old war house, our only choice of shelter. We spent a good share of one day collecting firewood and a lot of slabs and poles to patch the crevices of our refuge. These, with a couple of buffalo hides which we fortunately had saved to lay on the ground, sufficed with other skins to keep the snow from beating in, but we were most uncomfortable for the smoke would not pass out, the surging storm beating it back.

Toward morning of the third day the storm gradually died down and by daylight it was clear and still, with zero weather. The safety and whereabouts of our ponies was our first consideration. We knew that in a storm they would travel with it to the first sheltered coulee or ravine and our course, therefore, was to travel in the wake of the late storm and scan the country ahead for signs, for the drifting snow had obliterated all tracks. Presently we saw them feeding in a wind-swept flat above a timbered hollow, where they had no doubt taken shelter.

On our return we went out of our way to look at a bait in a gulch, but before we got to it we came upon some fresh moccasin tracks made that morning in the snow and coming from the direction of our camp. As they made but one track, each following in the footprints of the foremost man, we judged that there were not less than four or five people. They held a long stride and were in a hurry. We immediately took the back trail to see how things were at our camp, for we were anxious about our saddles and our spare ammunition.

The tracks kept closely to the gulches that led out from the creek bottom. About three hundred yards above our camp we found a war house that plainly showed recent occupation. Tracks were plain all about in the snow, and the interior indicated a hasty withdrawal. A pair of old moccasins of Sioux make and pieces of blanket used as foot wraps were still hanging on a line, and the fire in the center of the lodge was still warm.

The surroundings, taken in connection with a few shots that I had fired at a deer shortly after starting in the morning, told the story. There were no tracks anywhere except around the lodge. This said plainly that the inmates had come there during the last night's storm and had stumbled upon this old war house as a means of shelter. The wind and snow had swept away all traces of their approach. On hearing my rifle shots they had made a hasty departure, fearful, no doubt, of an instant attack. As for us, we were thankful that the storm had concealed us from our undesirable neighbors.

After this experience we kept a better lookout. Our horses were not allowed to wander from camp, and in three days we were on the trail again toward the Musselshell, leaving the usual notice to inform our partners, whose return we expected any day now, of our probable whereabouts.

In a couple of days we were together again. Erwin and his companion had had their experiences also. They were caught in the storm without any fresh meat and there was no killing any until the storm was over. In the interval Mike shot a coyote and undertook to see how the meat would go boiled. When the pot had boiled the usual length of time he fished out a piece and chewed on it awhile, but it was either too tough to masticate or the stomach rebelled, or perhaps the merriment of his partner interfered with the destined course of the choice morsel. The pot was again put to service on the coals and a fresh burst of cooking rendered the meat more tender, if not more palatable; Mike managed to swallow a piece, and thereupon set up a howl in simulation of a wolf, to the great amusement of the one onlooker. Thus is the strenuous life relaxed and relieved. Erwin and Mike ran onto an old she-bear suckling two well-grown cubs. The dressed meat of the cubs they brought with them, and most delicious meat it was, just like young pig, a great seasoning for the lean meat of that season.

The party now being together again, we proceeded to the Musselshell, where we collected a number of wolf-skins, and tacking down those that were green, cached those that were not dry enough to pack under a pile of brush near our camp. Taking advantage of thawing weather, we now retraced the course already traveled, skinned the wolves we had piled in the vicinity of the baits, and with such loads as could be carried made for the cabin in the Cone Butte Pass.

We found everything just as we had left it, our hides

133

and furs having been cached in the crevices under the shelves of sandstone that lined the hillside near our cabin. The skins of elk, deer, wolf, and fox soon covered the ground in process of airing and drying; fresh skins and those only part dry were repegged. This task consumed about a week, when we packed our horses again and set out to clean up our winter's work.

When we arrived at the Musselshell River we found that the snow had fallen during our absence and there were many old footprints made by Indians around our camp. On looking around we found a newly constructed war house in the pines, a great green tepee covered very cleverly with pine boughs. We were certainly fortunate to have missed the party that built it, for it was a large one.

Our good fortune in avoiding Sioux war parties was a subject of frequent remark. Of course we used all proper measures to attain that end. A collision with the Sioux might spell disaster, or interfere seriously with our enterprise of gathering valuable furs and skins. We were not bloodthirsty, and if they would let us alone we were willing to give them the road. It was only when they were viciously inclined and aching for a fight that we met them halfway. For that reason we used our skill and knowledge to keep out of their way, though we often suffered discomfort in doing it.

On the way back we camped for a day or two on a creek that is marked McDonald's on a map before me of the state of Montana bearing the date of 1911 and filled out in counties with a maze of streams, towns, and railway lines, to say nothing of parks, game preserves, and reservations. This creek, bank-full of snow water, did not show any signs of beaver dams or houses but seemed to be alive with beaver, of which we killed a number, recovering more after the water had subsided, for a beaver will sink if not killed instantly.

When we were ready to leave Cone Butte Pass the season had advanced and for some reason it was decided to go to Reed's place in the Judith Basin before returning to Carroll. I remember camping at a beautiful spring near a running stream and I am told that the city of Lewiston now covers this ground. The war parties were very active that spring of 1876, and on the way across the mountain we had crossed a fresh horse-trail at right angles to our course, made by a party of a hundred or more. We heard from this war party a couple of days later.

From Reed's cabin the prairie stretched clear for a mile to some rising ground, over which the trail to Carroll had its way. Some friendly Indians had encamped near the trade store and let their bands of horses stray near these foothills nearly a mile away, when suddenly there was a cry, "The Sioux! the Sioux!" and rushing out I saw a cavalcade of Indians, fifty or more, sweeping along the edge of the prairie at an easy gallop with the evident intention of cutting out the pony herd. Our own horses were safe in the opposite direction and while my companions hastened to secure them I kept on at a smart run in the direction of the pony herd, which seemed to be without a guard. I was soon joined by a young Indian from the lodge.

My intention was to come as near the pony herd as possible and get in a few long-distance shots at the Indians before they reached it. The war party, however, paid no attention to us nor did they quicken their pace, but for all their indifference I surmised a keen calculation as of experts in the business of stealing horses. When they started to round up the stock and turn it toward the foothills I sat down and pumped at them as they came into line or bunched, but I could see no result except a scattering when I fired at three who happened to be close together. The young Indian with me never stopped, and when the thieves disappeared over the hill with the band of horses he was still on the trail.

Not being able to dispose of our skins and furs to advantage in the Judith Basin, we made our way to Carroll and unloaded in the enclosed ground of the principal trader, spreading our stuff out to air and dry, and also for inspection. The other trader, Clendenning, bid on the skins, but the price did not come up to our expectations. Meanwhile, the Missouri was rising rapidly and the chocolate-colored flood was encroaching on the bank at the rate of thirty or forty feet a day. The river bank was less than a hundred feet away and the force of the current seemed to concentrate at that point. When the corner of the stockade threatened to dispense with its foundation we moved our furs and skins back, and had moved them a second time when the forces of the flood called a halt and ate great slices of the bank lower down.

At this stage, to our great satisfaction, an up-river steamboat put in and a buyer from St. Louis agreed to our price. Prime wolf-skins were worth five dollars each, but I do not recall now what beaver and other furs brought. I know that the check went to the trader and there was a snug little sum left to divide among the four hunters after he had deducted for his merchandise. I had only to saddle my pony and lash my belongings on the pack horse and I was ready for the trail. I did

Hunting in the Judith Basin

not remain long in Carroll. The lovely hills and valleys called me.

I remember that instead of taking the old wagon road that connected Carroll with the Judith Basin I selected at random a point of ridge, for I liked to go by devious ways, if feasible, and never the same course twice. This brought me to the open country much to the right of my direct road. I could look back and see a maze of ridges and backbones, all trending toward the Missouri. I remembered the ridge where the Indian warrior, creeping and trailing the phantom deer as they fed and lured him from bush to denser shrubbery, was struck down by a mountain lion which, slinking in the dusk of ebbing twilight to intersect the same quarry, saw with baleful vision his evening meal stalking beside him, leaped on the instant and struck a mighty blow, and sped away at contact with man.

I rode along the wooded ridge, still colorful of late springtime, in the shade of stunted pines and cedars and the entire scene assumed shape in my mind and was reenacted in minute detail. I seemed to feel the concern of the warriors as the deer hunter failed to return. The little spots of camp fires shaded with green boughs were dimmed and darkness settled over the bivouac. I saw in the early morn the return of the scouts who had nothing to report; a hasty conference, instant separation, and the hunt for sign in the difficult and much trodden ground began. In a series of circles they pick up the footprints of the hunter and the track of the lion. Where the lines converge they see a dark form; "That is he," they murmur; they gather up the cold and lifeless figure of the warrior, bear it to the rendezvous, and prepare it for burial; wrapped in his blanket, with his bow and arrows, his knife and gun, lashed to a light scaffold in a cedar tree, they give him to the ardent Sun God and the friendly stars.

Thus musing, I picked my way along the ridges till the rolling plain gave a view of the Judith Mountains, their slopes coming down to the plain in rough outline, but seeming smooth in the distance. I saw smoke rising from the valley and toward it I made my way, knowing that I would touch the road I had left.

From the road I turned again toward the smoke, for I saw lodges and knew that friendly Indians were encamped. I passed wrinkled old squaws splitting firewood from dry logs and stumps with axes that had seen better days. These Indians were strange to me and I inquired by sign. The sign they gave me was also strange, but when I pronounced the word "Piegan," they nodded and signed me to alight and eat. Though I saw no preparations for a meal and no sign of buffalo meat in camp, the pursuit of which, I learned, had brought them here, I was nothing loath to eat when invited and so I dismounted, taking my bridle off to let my pony graze where he would. One of the women brought a stew of meat and gave me a portion in a wooden dish. It tasted good, but I am sure that it was not buffalo, elk, or deer meat. I had a suspicion what it was, but not the heart to question.

I wandered my way along the foothills of the Judith, where wild strawberries bloom and ripen, and in the course of time looked down on the basin and afar off saw the white tents of a military encampment in grassy ground a little way above Reed's cabin.

CHAPTER IX

CAMPAIGNING WITH GENERAL MILES

TURNING aside from my projected trip to the Gallatin Valley, I headed for the Flat Willow country and was soon jogging down one of the numerous game trails that follow water courses. Small game, such as deer and antelope, were pretty well scattered at this season and the buffaloes had mostly moved north, but a few were still coming from the direction of the Yellowstone, caused probably by the movements of troops and the restless activity of the redskins in that region. I felt satisfied that no war parties would take the field against the river Crows or the Blackfeet while soldiers were in the Yellowstone Valley, and that therefore it was reasonably safe for a lone hunter to travel across country. If not safe, I must take the chances and whatever followed.

My usual caution deserted me, though, when a big black bear jumped from his resting place and went loping swiftly up a smooth ridge, covering ground awkwardly but with the speed of a more nimble animal. I jumped from my horse, intending to see how close I could place a bullet without hurting him. The bullet struck the ground close to one of his hind legs, raising a little spot of dust. As quick as a flash bruin struck the spot with a mighty whack of one of his paws. I seemed to hear it, and believe I did, but I may have been like the denizen of the Arctic, who, watching the aurora borealis, seems to hear a rustle when the mighty curtains, flaming in color, fold and unfold in wonderful action across the sky, but if his eyes be closed, cannot.

But for my curiosity to see a bear jump and hasten his stride, I might not have fallen in with John Stanwix and his party of five, trappers all, for I had proceeded but a little way when I saw three riders, who had just emerged from a grove of pines and stood fixed in their tracks, gazing intently in my direction. As I approached, three more riders came out of the wood with pack ponies, the sight of which caused my own pack pony, which followed loose behind my saddle mare, to prick up his ears and forge ahead.

One of the three who had watched my approach rode a little way to meet me. He was a soldierly-looking man of about thirty-five years, with a pair of keen, dark eyes set under a soft brown hat, and I remember that he wore a woolen shirt of drab with a rolling collar, and that a light rifle in a short, stiff leather case was attached under his leg to the saddle.

"I am John Stanwix," he said, "and I know that your name is Kelly, for I have seen you before. Where are you now bound for?"

"Mr. Stanwix, I am glad to meet you," I replied, "I am headed for the valley of the Yellowstone, but I have a notion that I may camp with you this night."

"Good," he rejoined, "stick to that notion. I would like nothing better. May I ask what you were firing at just now?"

The rest of the party had dismounted and were tightening and rearranging packs as we approached. Several nodded to me, and one chap who would take the prize on red hair, asked: "Where is your bear? I sure heard one whine after that shot."

"Oh, it was a happy miss," I said. "Poor fur and little fat on an old she-bear this time of year."

We sat on the grass and smoked and some mention was made of General Custer's fight with the allied Sioux, accounts of which had dribbled in by way of the Gallatin Valley. When "Stan," as they called the leader, mounted his horse we all took leather and pushed on to the Musselshell, where, as I learned, they had cached some prospecting tools earlier in the season.

At night around the camp fire there was more talk about the fight on the Little Big Horn, and it appeared that Stanwix knew a whole lot about the Sioux and could talk the language quite fluently. I surmised that he was familiar with the Sioux agencies in the lower country. In his opinion this was the last combined rally of the non-agency Indians. Their choice hunting grounds, extending from the Black Hills on the south to the Canadian border and beyond on the north, were about to be invaded by a railroad, and that meant disaster and loss to what the Indian valued most.

"Personally," he said, "I am not painfully distressed over the outlook, for now" (picking up a battered gold pan and drumming on it), "we can go where we like to prospect, without hiding out from the redskins."

Turning to me, he said: "A short time before we made this cache, we had an odd experience with a war party of Sioux and Cheyenne. The party is complete with the exception of one who is not with us now." I remember that one or two of the party chuckled, and the red headed man, who wore no hat and was called "Vance," said, "And I reckon, Stan, that Crow boy is running yet."

"Yes," replied Stan, "that Crow was going to show

us gray quartz on the Musselshell that had little specks of gold all through it.

"Well, we were piking along somewhere this side of Wolf Gulch or Wolf Spring when we ran plumb on to four Indians afoot, packing a big bundle between them. Then we saw just ahead four mounted Indians, each leading or driving a pony. We headed for them and you may be sure they saw us on the instant, and putting down the bundle ran to join the others but not before they gave a couple of war whoops, whereupon one of the mounted men discharged his musket in the air. Then we saw quite a party ahead riding slowly, but they turned, and scattering out came flying in our direction. I waved those nearest us to stop, and called out in Sioux that we were heart good. They turned immediately and rode toward us and I saw that the bundle they had carried was alive, and, as I had suspected, a wounded Indian.

"By this time the main party, about twenty in number, were almost upon us and I waved them to halt, shouting: 'Do not come nearer than the hill; we are white men and will see what can be done for this man.'

"The Crow, who was helping to keep the packs on the trail in the rear, at first sight of the Indians turned and skipped and we saw him no more.

"Handing my rifle to Jim, here, and cautioning all to keep a watch all around and wave back any Indians who tried to get closer, I told the Indians to unwrap the cover and take off the bandages so that I could examine the hurt. Two of them proceeded to do this, while the other four stood a little way off with the horses. The Indians on the hill dismounted, letting their ponies graze.

"I had a small bundle of medicine in a pack and the men brought a canteen of water. As the Indians unrolled the cover I saw that the sick man's leg was wrapped with an entire paunch case of an elk taken, probably, fresh and smoking hot from the animal. Nothing, to my notion, could have been better to allay swelling and inflammation. But what a sight! They had cut off the thick parts of the paunch and whipped out the contents and wrapped it around the shattered limb while it was still hot and moist.

"The steam from the hot skin, together with the gastric juice that may have adhered to the lining of the stomach of the elk, probably played their part in an effort to aid nature in restoring and making good a torn and crushed limb, but I do not know; I am not a surgeon. Anyway, there was no pus, though the knee was crushed and the small bones were protruding. Meanwhile, a fire had been built and water was heating, awaiting which I busied myself in removing loose bones while the Indian, a young man, regarded me with quiet eyes. Pointing to the knee, I asked how many sleeps, and he held up three fingers, but to my question what caused it, he closed his eyes, and another Indian answered for him, 'Blackfeet.'

"The water being now at a boiling point, I tore apart an old cotton shirt that Jim had in readiness, and passing it through the water wrung it out and washed the wound as well as I could, then dusted common baking soda on the torn flesh. The Indians brought dry willows and I made an attempt at splints, but it was a poor job.

"Finally, with a stiff piece of *manta,* off the packs, and the improvised splints we bound up the leg. Meanwhile, one after another of the Indians that stood by would go to the main party on the hill, and another would return in his place, I suppose to see what was going on. I asked the one who helped me what they proposed to do with this man, and he answered: 'He is my brother. We will carry him to a safe place that we have in view and I shall stay with him until he dies or is able to travel.'

"There was not a saddle in the party. They had been away more than a year on this foray, visiting Santee and Assiniboin and other friendly tribes, and whatever saddles they had had or accumulated must have been lost or disposed of before they struck the pony herds of the Blackfeet.

"I let them have one of our old pack saddles, as our packs were getting light, and instructed them to make a strong litter and fasten one end low down on each side of the saddle, then two men could easily hold the other ends and walk along at a good gait without jarring the sufferer much, also to loosen the canvas-bound leg if it swelled, and bathe it with warm water, and if the leg got 'bad' to kill a deer and wrap it as before. I also gave them some of the soda, as that was the best thing I had for cleansing a wound. Though I had a bottle of good liquor I judged it too good for an Indian, and gave him, instead, a dose of pain-killer, of which I had several bottles.

"While we were shifting packs and repacking, four Indians rode away in search of dry poles for a stretcher that could be fastened to a horse. And so we left them and pursued our way to the Musselshell, but we found no trace of quartz with yellow specks in it, and do not know to this day whether the Crow meant beyond the

Musselshell, in the Little Rocky Mountains, where, I am informed, good colors may be found, but no ledges, or farther still, to the Bear Paw Mountains. Anyhow, we had our travel for nothing."

I suspected that Stanwix and his crowd had passed the winter somewhere between the Snowy Mountains and Emigrant Gulch, the other side of the Yellowstone, while we were hunting wolves in the country bordering the Judith Basin, but did not ask, since they chose not to impart information as to their movements other than as given in the adventure above related.

They were frank and agreeable in all other matters, and on their part asked no questions. I put them down as Southerners, perhaps from the Texas border; however, my curiosity concerning them was only mildly alive, being content with their good fellowship. A chance remark that was made about "Hunter's Springs," and "Whitmore's Basin" led me to suspect that they intended to strike the Yellowstone higher up than I intended, but I would go along if they desired my company, knowing that I would not lack for company when once I reached the river.

Next morning while drinking our coffee and testing the contents of a Dutch oven well filled with fried meat, Stanwix said: "Kelly, we are going to hit the high places for the Yellowstone today, and it may be higher up the river than you want to go. I hope that you will keep right along with us."

"Well," I answered, "if you will let me off somewhere near the mouth of the Big Horn I shall feel at home." I got out my supply of sugar, coffee, salt, and flour and divided with them, saying that I had enough to last until I struck some military camp.

"Yellowstone Kelly"

Somewhere below Pompey's Pillar I left my chance acquaintances, who wended their way up the river while I pursued my course in the opposite direction on a well-worn road. By the time I reached the mouth of the Big Horn I met and passed wagons going down with supplies, and a wagon train going up the Yellowstone accompanied by detachments and units returning to their stations in the mountains. I remember one or two camps of soldiers between the Rosebud and Tongue rivers, temporary camps awaiting orders, or getting ready to march with Crook across the Black Hills.

I did not follow the windings of the river or I might have run into other organizations, but at the mouth of the Powder there was considerable stir, for Crook was getting his cavalry in shape to follow the retreating Sioux, whose trails led to the breaks of the Little Missouri River. Steamboats were in evidence and I am not sure if I did not meet again my old friend, Captain Grant Marsh of the *Far West*. I know that at the Powder I ran across Vic Smith, who was already a prominent and valuable scout attached to some of the expeditionary forces.

When the military cantonment at the junction of the Tongue and Yellowstone rivers was in process of building, I was on my way up Yellowstone Valley intending to return to Judith Basin, when I fell in with some Montana miners and prospectors traveling down stream. The news these men had caused me to change my mind about going to the Basin and to turn back with them to the new camp, which I now learned was under the command of General Miles.

With one of these men I turned aside to hunt in the cedar hills on the north side of the valley, where we ran upon a very large cinnamon bear, which at once put up a ravine. My companion and I separated, he going to the left and I to the right, though I saw no justification in shooting a bear at that season of the year. Presently I saw Mr. Bear only a few yards off in a hollow, and I plugged him with a .40 caliber bullet. He lurched and fell, tried to get up again, and fell dead. While I stood near his head regarding him, my companion returned and dismounting, fired point-blank at the head of the already dead animal, saying, "You can never tell when a bear may revive and rush one." I suspected, however, that his chief desire was to be in at the killing. When we overhauled the cinnamon he proved to be very fat. We estimated that several hundred pounds of fat covered his back and sides and that he would weigh ten or twelve hundred pounds, or perhaps more. The fur was poor and thin and of little value. I contented myself with taking a generous slab of back fat, one of his big paws, and the remaining claws, and then I had a load that was disagreeable to both the pony and his rider.

In those days the valley of the Yellowstone held some grand bottom lands with groves of cottonwood with grassy prairies between; and where the shallows of the river swept around were thickets of tall willows where the deer and elk loitered in the heat of the day, and the Indian came for material to build his sweat house or bull boat. The beautiful land is still there, but it is now fenced in and the romance and the wild life are gone forever.

Down the valley we rode, ever on the watch for game movements, for fresh trails crossed in every direction. At last we arrived near the site of the military cantonment, situated on an open plain on the south side of the river, about a mile above the junction of Tongue River. Crossing on a rude ferry operated by soldiers, we found the camp nearly deserted. Only Captain Randall, quartermaster, was visible, and he, good soldier and responsible officer, was looking after his property. We got acquainted without much ceremony; the soldiers were off in the woods cutting timbers for use in building quarters for the command and cover for supplies, and General Miles was along with the working parties.

Captain Randall noticed the big bear's paw hanging from my saddle. He smiled and said, "That's about as big as they make them, is it not?" I slipped the paw from the saddle leather and held it up; it was over a foot long without the claws.

"The General will want to see you," said the Captain. "He is curious to learn all he can about this country."

I still held the cinnamon's right hand aloft, having in mind to give it to him, but I said, "I will send it up as my card."

Captain Randall called an orderly and sent the paw to the General's tent with my compliments. After he had returned from the forest and learned who had left the card he sent for me. I walked over to the camp and tapped at his tent door. He bade me enter.

I had met him but once before and then only casually while with Vic Smith, the scout, whose acquaintance I had made one day at Powder River while observing the stir and confusion incident to drawing rations and supplies, for Crook was to begin his march to the Black Hills in the morning. While standing there General Miles rode up and accosted Vic Smith. Any picture of Miles at that period will show him in the full vigor and flush of manhood. He had an eye for details, and noticing something loose about Vic's bridle he leaned over and adjusted it while Vic said, deprecatingly, "Oh, never mind, General."

The General questioned me about the country north of the Yellowstone and as far as the British line, its accessibility as a field for operations against hostile Indians, and the location and disposition of the Sioux toward the north, all of which I answered to the best of my ability, having roved for years in parts of that region, hunting, trapping, and "standing off" bad Indians. The country just north of the mouth of the Tongue River and beyond the valley of the Yellowstone as far as the Missouri was little known to me, however, or to anyone who lived in the country at that period. It had been given over to the Sioux and their allies and was a blank on any map available. Before our interview came to a close I was impressed with the fact that General Miles had in view considerable fall and winter campaigning, not forgetting hunting trips as a source of relaxation.

I wended my way to the camp of my hunter friends near the river, where I found a cozy camp fire under the cottonwoods. I was now chief scout for the district of the Yellowstone.

Not many days had passed when I received instructions to proceed north to the Milk River country to learn what I could about certain semi-hostile Sioux reported to be encamped on or near Frenchman's Creek in the heart of a great buffalo region. Nearly all of the country to be traversed was a great game country and choice buffalo range, dominated in part by the different bands of Hunkpapa, Teton, Oglala, and Yankton, who were jealous of encroachments by other Indians. No white man in my time had gone through that region.

My intention was to strike straight across country for Fort Peck, opposite the mouth of the Big Dry, on the Missouri. It was a long, lonesome trip and I asked that Vic Smith be detailed to accompany me, as two pairs of eyes were better than one. General Miles gave me a note to Colonel Otis, who was in command of a station on the lower Yellowstone near Glendive Creek. Vic was his guide and scout. It was really an imposition on my part to deprive the Colonel of his services, but I had to have someone of experience on such a perilous trip.

I rode down there and we made a little pack of bacon, flour, sugar, and coffee to tie on our saddles. Late in the afternoon we stopped at headquarters to bid the Colonel good-by. As I remember it, this station was but a military camp of white tents, pitched convenient to the river bank. Colonel Otis was a very pleasant gentleman, whom I remember meeting but once again on the road to Bismarck, Dakota, when Joseph and the remnant of the Nez Percés were en route under guard to the states in the following year.

Colonel Otis said, "I wish you a successful trip, but I have not the slightest idea where you are going."

I told him that we purposed crossing the Missouri near the Fort Peck trading post, and that the information received there would probably govern our further movements before returning directly to the Tongue River cantonment.

As we left the broken country bordering the Yellowstone and approached the low divide that looks down upon dry water courses that give to the Missouri we exercised more caution. I had an excellent pair of heavy field glasses of that day, which I had obtained a short time before from one of General Terry's teamsters in exchange for a pony. As he gave me my choice of a mule or the glasses I surmised that they were contraband of war, as both were the regulation article. However, the government charges such losses to accidents in the service, or to a battle, and Jake Gordon, teamster, was probably aware of the fact.

It was now night, with no moon and the sky only partly clear. I had never before been in that part of the country. Nevertheless, we continued on far into the night, as long as we could see. We had encountered no timber since leaving the Yellowstone, excepting here and there a scraggly cottonwood, but now before us was a low plain dotted with shrubbery and a shimmer of water. Was this a mirage of the night? We stepped carefully toward it and the whole thing melted away as a band of buffaloes and their near friends, a cloud of white antelopes, slipped out of sight.

Farther on we came to the edge of a ridge and could see far down, seemingly into a park of scattered timber. The descent appeared precipitous. "Here is where we walk," I said, as we dismounted. Leading our horses we stepped over the edge and in a few yards found ourselves on a little flat covered with sage brush that the night had magnified into big trees afar off. Traveling across country over unfamiliar ground on a night not too clear is trying to the nerves, and we made our way slowly, routing out buffaloes that were invisible to us, but indicated by our horses pricking up their ears and changing gait a trifle. They could see pretty well in the night, but for us the rumble of hoofs, the odor of warm bodies, and the light skim of dust that held in the air was convincing enough.

After midnight we halted in a place which seemed to be secluded from observation, where there was a little grass. Picketing our mounts, we sought out a smooth spot where we placed our saddles and rolling our blankets about us slept until the sun was up. It is hard to find a place in the night that is not exposed to view from some point, and ours proved no exception. Nevertheless, we dared not move for fear of alarming the buffaloes that were all about, which would quickly draw attention if any Indians happened to be in the vicinity. According to my reckoning we were not far from Big Dry Creek. If correct, we could reach that stream lower down by following the tributary on which we were encamped. About noon we started down the gulch and after watering our horses made good time to Big Dry, where we ascertained that the trails had not been used by horsemen lately, and, satisfied that the coast was clear, rode rapidly on, reaching the mouth late in the afternoon.

I found some changes at Fort Peck since my last visit, when en route with Broadwater's ox train to Carroll, on the upper river. An agent of the Interior Department was in charge and a class of young Indians was in process of formation for instruction. What a change! Gone was the romance of the trader, trapper, hunter! Enter the new order of education! A trim and pleasant-faced gentleman gave us a bed to sleep in. Heretofore you spread your blanket, or perhaps requisitioned a buffalo robe from the storeroom for your bed, on the puncheon floor, and made a roll for a pillow.

This teacher engaged us in conversation and spoke of plans for the welfare of the red man. I told him that if the plans of the district commander on the Yellowstone were carried out more than one camp of hostile Indians would be settled in the valley where the soil was rich and would need instruction in cultivating the ground as soon as confidence and good feeling were once established. I was dipping into the future somewhat, but all this came to pass in less than a twelvemonth, for the Sioux and Cheyenne whom we fought at Wolf Mountain came out of the hills and made peace with General Miles at the military camp near Tongue River on the Yellowstone.

I missed the old-time cook, George Cooley, who was an artist at compounding dishes in which meat formed the principal part. When stormy weather had dispersed the game to their sheltered haunts and fresh meat was lacking, he made stews of pemmican of an alluring flavor. The factor would send favored Indians to George, who would serve them meat and coffee and sometimes bread, if they had rich furs to trade, for real bread was a luxury in those days.

We learned that there were no permanent camps of hostiles north of the river, and what few Indians had drifted from the main camps were safely north of the line. We returned to Tongue River in due time by another route, I think by the Red Water and Flagg Creek, where no water is, but much mountain sheep sign.

About October 15 came a courier from Colonel Otis' command telling of an attack by hostiles on a wagon train en route for Tongue River. At once preparations were made to take the field and I looked any moment for an order to go somewhere, but none came. The wagon master got his train together, the commissary was issuing rations, and the ordnance officer looked after his fieldpieces. Finally, General Miles with part of his command crossed the Yellowstone and took the road leading northwest along the river. Somewhere about Sunday Creek he called me up and directed me to take some scouts and make a night march and ascertain if the Indians had left their camps below on the river, or were still in hiding. It was assumed that their camps were not far away and it was desirable to know if they were encamped where it was feasible to approach them, though my own opinion was that if they were on the north side of the river they could easily recross and harass any force that might attempt to use the same ford. Anyway, it meant a night ride on a moonless night, as I well remember, across a rough country, some of it like the bad lands in character.

I had four scouts besides "Billy," a half-breed, who was of much use to me in reaching the point I aimed at. We traveled on and on under the misty stars, stopping at times at ridges and ravines to examine trails for lodge-pole tracks. In the early hours of the morning it became darker. We were now near the wooded valley which infringed sharply upon the foothills, or bluffs, we had crossed. A well-traveled trail led along and soon turned off into short brush which had been cleared, and here was the site of an Indian village that had been abandoned but a short time before, as the lodge fires had left the ground still warm under them. We examined the ground as hastily as we could and noted that there were two camps in this place, one where the lodges were pitched without order and one in which the tents were arranged in a circle, indicating the presence of a party of Cheyenne.

With General Miles

Some of the horses were pretty well used up. The Indians had gone and we must be sure to pick up the main trail at first streak of dawn. I looked at my watch and said, "We will rest here one hour." In a moment every man tied his horse to brush or willow, and lying down where we were, sleep came at once, as though we were on a bed of spruce boughs.

At the very first streak of dawn we were up and looking for the trail, which was found with difficulty, and we sped along, men and horses greatly refreshed by the short rest. The air was calm and cool; as the morning changed from semi-darkness to light the outlook ahead presented a stretch of ridges to a divide that seemed a long way off. Each point was searched for some form of life, but there was nothing moving that could be seen, only a bare country of brown and yellow grass and low shrubs that struggled for existence.

Before we reached the divide the boom of artillery was heard at intervals, indicating that some fighting was going on. We pressed on, eager to learn how the fight was faring, and to take part in it if possible. Before we reached the top of the divide horsemen could be seen circling on the far hills, and as we got higher there lay before us a wide, treeless valley of yellow grass, on the farther slope of which a small train of army wagons moved slowly toward the ridge, while on either side a line of soldiers afforded protection against the Indians, who were darting and circling on two sides of the train and exchanging fire with the troops, who were firing at will whenever a mark presented itself. The main column marched in front and a rear guard behind.

The command was over a mile away, but we dashed down from the divide full tilt toward the train, for there was no other way of approach without making a wide detour on our back course, a change which did not commend itself at that moment. The Indians paid little attention to us until we had got to the dry water-course in the center of the flat valley, thinking perhaps that we were a part of reinforcements coming to their aid. Then they turned upon us while we were trying to keep out of the way of the burning prairie grass, but we easily drove them back. The valley was now hazy with smoke; only the rear guard was visible, and they seemed farther off than they really were, as we rode toward them, when suddenly they fired a volley point-blank at us.

Hardly had the bullets ceased to whine over our heads, or the smoke to roll from the rifles of our sharpshooter friends, before we had taken to cover. I went to the right under a bank, my companions to the left in a ravine. My thirst was so great at this moment that seeing a pool of water in front of me, just beyond a roll of prairie fire, I dashed through it, and falling flat, drank until my thirst was allayed. Returning to the friendly bank that had sheltered me, I peeped over and saw the rear guard, each man bent over and carrying his gun at a trail, advancing cautiously toward the spot where they supposed they had dispatched or placed *hors de combat* the too eager hostiles, who a moment before were pressing on their front so confidently. A non-commissioned officer was in advance, and when he came near I raised up and called to him. As soon as he saw me he turned to those behind him and called out, "Men, it's the scouts!"

My companions were little pleased with our adventure, and thought that I displayed unseemly glee at being subjected to a fusillade at such close quarters. Of course if the atmosphere had been clear, instead of being hazy with smoke, these soldiers never would have missed us. They were not shooting for fun and I blessed the gods that watch over careless folks. I made my way to the head of the column, which had halted, and General Miles smiled as he greeted me.

The hostiles, seeking to detain the troops while their people encamped beyond the hills were making a hurried retreat back to the Yellowstone, now left us, and the pursuit took the broad trail which the Indians could not hide, though the grass had been fired with the purpose of effacing it. The command encamped without turning aside from the trail.

Some time in the night a soldier awakened me from sound sleep, saying the General wished to see me. I found him with his staff of officers lying on the ground, wrapped in their military cloaks and blankets. The General questioned me at some length regarding the distance to the river, the fords, probable course of the fleeing Indians, and other matters that I do not remember now, though I have a vivid recollection that the night was clear and cold and while all around the ground was covered with sleeping bodies the commander was awake and taking measures for the coming day's work.

As usual, the scouts were ahead of the column. We came to the bank of the Yellowstone about noon that day, on an open, grassy bottom, the Indian trail leading to the ford a few hundred yards above. By direction of the General, Lieutenant Bailey of the Fifth Regiment went to examine the ford and I accompanied him. I think there were two or three soldiers along. I rode part way across the channel at the deepest point in order to demonstrate to the onlookers that the ford was feasible and easy if a fellow did not mind wading in cold water to his waistline, about forty feet on a gravelly bottom. It shallowed to the farther bank, but I hesitated about going over, not knowing how many redskins might be concealed in the low fringe of willows that garnished the sand bar.

Indians were seen in the woods at this place before we returned to the waiting command, and I was expecting an order to take the scouts and see what kind of hornet's nest we could stir up on the farther bank, when an Indian rode into view, bearing a pole with a white rag attached, and halloed across the water.

I am not sure whether Billy, the half-breed, acted as interpreter during the parley that ensued, or whether that fine interpreter and man, John Brughier, served in this capacity. Anyway, the Indians responded to an invitation to talk and came over in numbers. Some did not come direct to meet the officers, but circled around like wild creatures suspicious of a trap. Finally, the leading men sat down in a half-circle on the yellow grass, facing General Miles and his officers. With the soldiers hovering in the background and the October sun above casting light and warmth, the group made an interesting and striking picture.

One incident I recall clearly. Gall, the cunning fellow, did not come in with the rest of the chiefs, but after the conference had started he crossed the river alone and took his seat with the rest in the circle. Hard-tack had been passed around, and Gall, taking four in his hand, took a big bite out of all four like a hungry man. Some point of interest being stated, he suddenly ceased munching with his jaws and listened intently, while a wild look shone in his eyes.

With General Miles

The parley ended by the Indians agreeing to go to their agencies, and to show their good faith they left several of their chiefs as hostages for the surrender of their people. The troops now returned to the cantonment on Tongue River.

CHAPTER X

A WINTER PURSUIT OF HOSTILE INDIANS

IT was not long before General Miles had another expedition organized and ready for field service. He had learned that part of the hostile Sioux had escaped north and knew that a winter campaign would bring them to terms or result in driving them so far north that they would cease to be a menace. This was hard on the troops, but still harder on the redskins, who were forced to live on the country and had no supply depot to fall back on.

Your wild Indian in order to live comfortably must camp where there is game and also grass for his pony herds and where the women can dress hides to barter for flour, cloth, powder and shell munition, salt, and sugar. So they slipped north to their old hunting grounds east of the Musselshell and along the Missouri and north of it, where they could scatter out safely.

Early in November we crossed the Yellowstone and headed for the unknown country of the Big Dry, a tributary of the Missouri that is not much of a watercourse during the dry season, but a great feeding ground for buffalo that come down out of the far north at the approach of winter and fill all the shelter ranges along the Bear Paw Mountains, Milk River, and the country south. Traders and half-breeds came down from the Canadian side and made robes in the Milk River region, and bought robes of the wild Indians on this side of the line. Occasionally the Indians could buy a little

A Winter Pursuit

Red River rum in exchange for robes and skins, a beverage that found much favor with them.

A crossing was made of the Missouri near Fort Peck. Here I was detached with a small party of scouts, with orders to go down the right bank of the river a certain distance in search of any camps of Indians that might have been delayed in joining the main camps said to be moving north, and then cut across country and overtake some troops who were to be detached from the main column to explore the forks of the Big Dry for hostile Indians. The command was well organized to encounter cold weather as well as Indians, and most of the men and officers, accustomed to service on the plains, were hardened to a high point of efficiency, willing and able to go anywhere.

We rode down the right bank of the Missouri while dark clouds gathered denoting a storm. Finally, it did snow heavily, covering all tracks, but we pushed on for there was no stopping until we had got beyond Wolf Point. Down in the bottom a dry cottonwood stump was burning and had melted the snow away, and here we found evidence of a small camp of three or four lodges of Indians, who had decamped leaving no trail, for the snow had covered it.

The air now being clear of snow, and not deeming it necessary to follow the river any longer, I left my companions to make a fire while I crossed the river to a small cabin or trading establishment to obtain what information I could regarding hostile Indians in the vicinity. This was a risky piece of business as there was water and slush on top of the ice. I therefore dismounted, and making a rough hackamore of the end of my lariat, led my horse, so that if the ice proved to be thin I could recover and either return or make a detour on firmer footing. It was dark before I had made my way through the woods to the buildings used for trading with the Assiniboin and other Indians that passed along the trails going to or returning from the north. I learned that three families had crossed the river that day, having been alarmed at the approach of the military down the Big Dry, of which they had been advised by relatives in the Sioux camp.

It was too dark to return that night across the river, though I feared that if the thawing weather continued there would be much water on the ice by morning. Nevertheless, I took the chance and spent a pleasant evening with these people, who confidently looked forward to the government at last taking the wild Indians in hand and establishing agencies for their betterment. In the morning an Indian boy showed me where the families had crossed, though the moving water had obliterated all signs. The boy said that the ice was *suta,* and offered to go ahead, but I shook my head, thinking that I would rather encounter the danger alone than have a boy, even an Indian boy, tackle it in my behalf. I pushed ahead without leading, as the water was clear and I could see that the ice was strong.

I found my companions ready to take the trail, and having decided that we had come far enough on our quest, which was now blocked by the cover of snow, without wasting time I led the way over the hills to join the expedition en route for the Big Dry, for they might be in need of our services if they went very far in that direction. We took the high ground so as to be able to see over the country for some distance, but the gray sky gave a somber cast to the uplands, on which the ante-

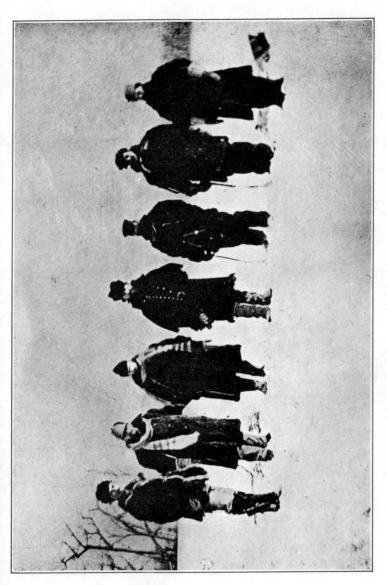

GENERAL MILES AND STAFF IN WINTER GARB, 1875-76

lopes trotting in a circle stood out clear and distinct against clay bank or drifted snow. We saw no other game, not even a slinking wolf or fox.

Late in the afternoon Jim Wood, one of the scouts, killed a two-year-old buffalo bull in a hollow where a few young cottonwoods gave promise of water seepage. Our horses were tired and hungry and we did not wish to appear on the skyline after a shot had been fired, so we went into camp. As soon as the saddles had been removed from the horses we took our light axes and cut down the green cottonwoods, and after removing the limbs, turned our animals to the trunks, which they began to nibble at once with gusto. There is a lot of nutriment in the green bark of the yellow cottonwood and horses munch it eagerly. Cattle will chew the buds and smaller limbs, but cannot gnaw the bark.

Our horses being provided for, we rustled dry brush and limbs for a fire, which was soon blazing with little or no smoke. We then fell to upon the buffalo carcass. First the tongue was deftly extracted; this went to the man who had dropped his quarry so conveniently within the limits of our camping ground. The hide was next removed, a careful operation where several knives were in juxtaposition. This also went to the killer, who spread it on the ground and carefully pegged it down, a soft and warm adjunct to blanket cover for a night's rest. Around the small camp fire men gathered with sharpened green saplings, garnished with strips of raw meat and ribs, and sought to smother the fire with drippings of fat, the odor of which carried on the night air to a greater distance than the light of the fire. Afterward coffee was made and then the fire was dimmed, for our hórses would scent an Indian or a wolf and give us timely notice.

We were off early next morning without breakfast. Coming to the Big Dry, we found that we were a little ahead of the trail, and circling around we found it faring up a more northerly branch, where we stayed a space for breakfast and to let the stock graze on the herbage. Following on, we came to where the land flattened out and saw on a far ridge a single horseman, but could not tell whether it was a white man or an Indian. Following the soldier trail, we came to some rough ground of washed ravines and cut banks on our left, and riding on, received a volley of musketry which startled our horses, and for a minute we had a hard time holding them. We saw five Indians running for dear life to shelter and before they reached cover gave them a volley, though it did not stop any of them. They were so close that we could see their breechclouts trailing behind them, and the feathers fastened in their hair. We raced up and down to find some place to come at these fellows, but the ground was too rough and broken to work in. They had been waiting for us in safe ground near the trail, knowing that we were bound to pass that way, and the man on the ridge no doubt advised them as to our movements.

As no one was hurt I thought it advisable that we push on and join the column ahead, which we found on one of the forks of the Big Dry. Learning that the officer in command expected to remain in that vicinity for a number of days, or as long as his supplies permitted, I made, at his instance, a trip to the divide north, to spy out the land and ascertain whether there was any movement of troops in that direction.

A Winter Pursuit

Not discovering anything to warrant going as far as the Missouri I returned to the command at the Big Dry, and the commander having determined to return to the cantonment at Tongue River, I led him by a way that would reveal any hidden camps of Indians that might have scouting parties out, such as the one that had fired into our party a few days back. The general course, however, led toward the Yellowstone, which we reached without further incident a few days later.

It now appeared by the latest information that the General purposed on his return trip to cross the Missouri somewhere below the mouth of the Musselshell River, and thus penetrate the favorite hunting grounds of the hostile Indians, attacking them or driving them toward other columns detached for the same purpose, and keeping them on the move in winter weather when they were least prepared for such a movement and harry them until they were in a mood to submit to the government. It was a well-laid plan, and was carried out with skill and resolution with a small body of troops, who traversed a great extent of country over unknown trails in a vast region but poorly mapped. The officer in command of the cantonment in the absence of General Miles directed me to return across country and make every effort to find the main column of troops still in the field. I took two scouts with me. On the second day while we were cooking our breakfast two shots came faintly on the wind, and taking horse we rode forward a mile when we saw the prints of two pairs of army shoes and the ground torn where a band of buffaloes had been disturbed. Farther on was a lift of smoke above a gulch, or narrow valley. When we worked around to get a better view there was disclosed a military force in process of breaking camp. It proved to be General Miles and his command, in very good trim after the arduous campaign, which was now nearing completion. The General received us with some satisfaction and inquired for the welfare of the column operating along the Big Dry. Soon afterward we struck the trail we had made and took our way to the cantonment.

Here, soon after our arrival, occurred one of the minor tragedies of the war. From the hostile camps near the head of the Tongue River came a small party of Indians. To their left lay the cantonment; to the right, the timber-fringed river, along which a few lodges of Crow Indians were encamped. They saw the Crow lodges but did not pause, confident, perhaps, that the nearness of the white soldiers would afford them protection. As they trotted along on their hardy ponies the Crows advanced with outstretched hands and under pretense of shaking hands pulled several off their ponies, shooting and stabbing them at the same time. The rest sped to the hills unpursued. It may be that they came to spy on the military, or perhaps to confer with them in order to propose a truce for the winter, which would have been much to their advantage if not offset by conditions hampering their freedom to hunt on their favorite buffalo grounds.

A few days later a party of thieving Indians drove off the beef herd from the outskirts of the cantonment. General Miles at once organized a force to follow the raiding party. In order to carry plenty of supplies, the transportation was increased by the addition of an ox train of wagons. A start was made in the last days of December, 1876, the scouts, as usual, in advance. The almost constant passage of buffaloes and Indian travois

BUFFALO HORN
BANNOCK INDIAN SCOUT

JOHN BRUGHIER
HALF-BLOOD SIOUX GUIDE AND
INTERPRETER

"LIVER-EATING JOHNSON"
INDIAN FIGHTER AND SCOUT

packs kept the trail smooth up and down water courses, so that the wagons had little difficulty in keeping up with the marching column, and we made very good progress up Tongue River until we came to a remarkable congregation of rude shacks, big and little, that lined one side of the valley.

These were built of slabs and poles, rocks, and turf set in heterogeneous fashion, as though a large party of Indians had suddenly been attacked and driven from their camp on a freezing night and in their flight had happened on this spot and built these shacks to keep from perishing. It seems quite probable that this was the village that General Mackenzie had attacked and destroyed earlier in the season. As we advanced up Tongue River the valley narrowed and we came to where a large camp had been abandoned a day or two before, for the ground was still warm where the tepee fires had been. This camp was a large one and extended for miles up the valley. The trail of the stolen cattle led to it, and some of them had been butchered there.

Next morning, where we crossed the river through the willows there was a strong smell of Indian tobacco in the still, cold air, and the fresh print of pony tracks indicated that the young men were keeping watch over the advance of the troops. I had with me the three Johnsons (one of whom was the celebrated hunter and frontiersman on whom rested the sobriquet of "Liver-eating Johnson"), Tom LaFarge, interpreter for the Crows, three young Crow men, and Buffalo Horn, a Bannock, who was one of the bravest Indians I have ever had anything to do with.

Soon after, one morning early, the ox drivers, assisted by two or three soldiers, were driving in the cattle

that had wandered, when they were attacked by a party
of hostiles and two of the soldiers were killed. We were
in the advance and turned back, but the Indians had disappeared. The command halted to bury the two soldiers. Their grave was dug on the trail so that the passage of the troops and wagons would obliterate any
sign of the burial. The scouts went ahead, and I think
that it was that night that we made a night march to the
Rosebud to ascertain if there were any camps on that
stream. No sign was apparent, so we returned to camp
about daylight.

That day we traveled farther than usual ahead of the
command and had gotten more than a mile when we
struck an open place in the timber where the winter sun
shone warmly. We stopped to rest without posting a
picket, and before we knew it every man was in a
drowse. The valley of the Tongue River had now narrowed to a wide gulch, pretty well timbered. On one
side the timber obscured the line of low bluffs; on the
other side it was more open and we could see the banks
above the gulch. While we were nodding (traveling all
night had beguiled us from paying strict attention to
business) the Indians were watching us from both sides,
and it was easy to signal from one side to the other.
They were creeping through the brush to attack us, and
had nearly reached a position where they could fire on
us without exposing themselves greatly when the three
Crow scouts and Buffalo Horn, from the column now
nearing, passed through our little opening, and riding
on to look for deer ran on to these hidden hostiles, who
fired point-blank at them and decamped at the instant.

The Crows retired, flat on their horses, with much
precipitation, but Buffalo Horn followed the attacking

party, closely supported by the white scouts, who pushed the Indians through the timber and over the ridge to where they seemed to be in great force. The command stopped and went into camp, the Indians, now fully in view, watching us from a point of rock. Before dark they went up the river and we saw no more of them until the next day. As we advanced the country ahead became rugged and elevated. We were getting close to the Wolf Mountains, out of which the Tongue River debouched.

The command halted and went into camp, while the scouts went ahead. There was a strong, cold wind and we stopped behind a cedar tree for shelter and conceal- ment while looking ahead. I took my field glasses from the case, and turning them in the direction of the wind- ing valley above, noted some figures moving in our di- rection. The Indians soon discovered them and said at once that people were approaching. When they came a little closer I saw by their peculiar swinging gait that some of the party were women, and I notified the In- dian scouts that they must not be harmed or startled, that we would show ourselves quietly to them and con- vey them to headquarters.

They continued to advance along the snow-covered trail, unaware, apparently, that their people had moved camp and were far above the Tongue River. I now saw there were three women, a boy, a girl, and a child. As they came within a few yards of the position we had taken we rode quietly out, making signs to them not to be alarmed. They stopped where they were and com- menced to cry. The Crows touched each gently with the coup stick and I motioned them to continue along the trail. They seemed rather above the average type, and though we questioned them in Sioux they made no response. I surmised that they were probably members of some prominent family who had been on a visit to some distant camp, and returning missed their people who were all around us. I reported to General Miles and they were kindly treated, a tent and food being provided for them.

Shortly after this there was another alarm of Indians. I routed out the four white scouts and we raced up the river again, the Crows and the Bannock not following. We soon saw four or five warriors showing themselves from behind the crest of a ridge. When we had attained the point where the women were found we could see ten or fifteen Indians behind the ridge awaiting our approach. Having the lead and thinking rapidly, I concluded the proper thing to do was to charge them. They were resting their guns on their crossed gunsticks and when we arrived within fifty yards some forty or fifty of them who had been concealed rose up and delivered their fire as we circled and returned the volley. The indifferent marksmanship of the Indians alone saved us. Tom LaFarge's horse was shot under him and another horse was disabled.

There was a little bunch of scrub oak in a hollow a short distance away and we made for it. To reach it we were compelled to jump our horses down a rocky shelf five or six feet to solid ground. All this time the Indians were firing away at us, the bullets striking the rocks and raising little dust patches from the ground. It was miraculous that no one was seriously hurt.

Arriving at the bunch of oaks, we quickly changed all this. Throwing the bridle reins down, our horses stood while we paid attention to the Indians, who were now scattered along the ridge and would pop up, but never in the same place twice, and without taking much aim blaze away at us. Whenever an Indian showed his head long enough to draw a bead on it he generally disappeared for good, but they were very shy of exposing themselves long enough for us to get a shot. They kept up a constant whooping to encourage each other and shifted their ground so as to surround us on three sides.

Our Indian scouts, who had tardily followed us, took up a position about two hundred yards away in the direction of the command and did good execution in keeping their side clear, but the Bannock, Buffalo Horn, who was with them, came riding up to us at this critical time as calmly and deliberately as though nothing had happened and took station near me.

Our enemy now numbered more than a hundred. There was a lull in the firing, an ominous lull. Pointing to the high bank just above us, I nodded to Buffalo Horn and together we dashed up it just in time to intercept three Indians who were stealthily approaching our retreat. Almost before we could fire at them they had worked out of sight in the most wonderful way. They seemed to fly along the ground, but I am confident that I made a hit in that flying exit of feathers, legs, and arms. The Indians now made it so hot for us at this point that I hastily returned to my companions, but Buffalo Horn, ignoring my call, secreted himself in some crevice and kept them off on that side.

It may be imagined that the command was not idle during this fusillade. Being informed of the firing, General Miles directed a detachment of soldiers under Lieutenant Hargous to proceed up the valley, but to beware of an ambush. At the same time the General ordered a shell fired at some Indians who could be seen on a hill near our position.

There was another lull in the firing, broken only by scattered shots, and we fully expected to be charged by the ever increasing body of Indians. Just then a shell came over our heads and exploded a little way beyond their line. This scattered and confused them somewhat, and gave us a chance to get to higher ground and fire a few more shots at them. We now saw the detachment of infantry marching rapidly in our direction; as it was now nearly dusk we got out of the place as quickly as we could, but no persuasion would bring the Bannock and it was long after dark when he reached camp. He hid behind a fallen tree and shot two of the Cheyenne as they followed the soldiers to camp.

All night the Indians surrounded the camp, and under an overcast sky some of them managed to creep close enough to communicate with the women prisoners, who cried out to them in answer to some shouted words in the Cheyenne language. Some shots were exchanged with the camp guards, then quiet settled down, for all lights were out. The Indians, seemingly, had retired, as was usual, to a distance to their bivouac, to await the dawn.

The military were astir very early the next morning and breakfast was served without delay. We were camped on the right bank of the Tongue River, and a bench above the edge of the camp formed a little mesa to a sloping bluff that extended to a ridge about four hundred yards distant. The bank leading to this ledge was about twenty-five feet high. Up this bank a field-piece was taken and planted in a position to resist attack, or to be held in reserve for any emergency.

A Winter Pursuit

The fighting soon became general on two sides; above in the timber, and across the stream, which at this point was shallow and small. The Indians closed in gradually, taking advantage of the convenient covering on all sides. But the soldiers also had excellent cover, of which they took advantage to drive the Indians from some of the positions they had attained. The firing now was fast and furious on both sides.

As this was a soldiers' fight, where the scout would find little freedom to exercise strategy in stealing upon the enemy without danger of being subjected to a cross fire from both sides, I became a mere spectator, so I took my place near the artillery on the bench, where General Miles stood with a little switch in his hand directing operations.

The fieldpiece was a target for some of the Indian marksmen, and the mules had been taken down from the hill, one of them having been shot. Indeed, a bullet struck one of the spokes of the wheel while I stood there. I got busy with my field glasses and searched every bush and tree within rifle shot for signs of the hidden marksmen, thinking that if I could locate the rascals I might by some artifice turn the tables on them, under the protection of the fieldpiece, before they did some serious harm.

But soon my attention was attracted to another point by the hasty gathering of a large force of horsemen in the upper part of the field for some demonstration. When they started I called General Miles' attention to the movement and he was quick to see that they were headed for the ridge within musket shot of the spot where we stood. Two companies were ordered to the summit to drive the Indians back. This force was led by

Majors Butler and Casey. As the troops labored up the steep ascent in the snow the Indians raced to anticipate them and arrived at the summit first. The General gave another order and presently I saw Captain Baldwin, with a box of rifle ammunition on the front of his saddle, riding to overtake the column. Certainly the box could not have been full for the weight would have taxed the strength of both horse and rider, but he made it manfully and when next I caught a glimpse of him he was waving his hat and urging the men on.

The Indians, having won the race to the summit, resorted to a ruse to draw the fire of the soldiers in the advance. The ridge was level and along it in full view the medicine chief of the party in full costume of feathered cloak and war bonnet danced for a space of forty yards in the most graceful and nonchalant manner. To the observer who understood the meaning of this action the different phases that assumed shape as the little drama proceeded were of absorbing interest. In his fate the Indians would read success or failure in their sally; if the magic of his charm worked he could not be killed, and supported by this demonstration his confederates would carry everything before them.

As soon as the soldiers arrived at the point where they could see the medicine man they stopped and commenced shooting at him. He paid no attention, however, but just danced along and when he got to the end of the path that he had apparently marked out for himself, he swung easily and danced to the other end. The longer he was the object of attention the faster the soldiers blazed away. But he did not stay long, for his pace subsided to a walk and finally he tottered and disappeared from view just as the Indians got into position to fire at the approaching soldiers, who took the ridge in storming fashion. Several warriors were killed or wounded in this skirmish, and as the soldiers mounted the crest of the hill the Indians were seen retreating down the ridges to the main body. They never rallied after this, but moved slowly up the river into the shadows of Wolf Mountain.

Snow had been falling for some time, yet General Miles followed the Indians with part of his command to make sure that they had left for good, and then returned to camp. The expedition now returned to the cantonment. The captive women were treated with the utmost kindness and after being held a month or two they were sent back to the hostile camp under charge of the half-breed interpreter, John Brughier, with a message to the hostile chiefs. Brughier, who was a very capable and trustworthy man, had lived in the hostile camp, having fled there to escape the officers of the law, who were after him on account of a misunderstanding he had had with a white man. At Cedar Creek he came over to General Miles and from that time had been identified with the military operations.

So Brughier and the three Cheyenne women traveled up the Tongue and across the hills to where the hostile Sioux and Cheyenne had made their camp near the Big Horn Mountains. Finally, all trails led in one direction to where herds of ponies grazed on snowy hills and along wooded gulches, and there young men came out to meet the travelers and escort them to their people. The result of this meeting and the message Brughier bore was to bring the leading warriors to the cantonment for a conference, where good feeling and confidence were established to such a degree that the major part of these warring people moved to the valley of the Yellowstone in the vicinity of the cantonment, where under the direction and care of the government they were taught the arts of peace and agriculture—truly a sudden change of life for a wild people. Subsequently, acting on the advice of friends, Brughier gave himself up to the courts, where he was defended by that brilliant genius of the law, "Bill" Erwin, the famous criminal lawyer of Minnesota, and cleared of the charge held against him.

It was now about twelve years since I had left home to enter the army in the closing year of the Civil War, and as everything seemed quiet on the border I broached to General Miles the subject of going east on a short trip; he was not averse, but said that he had in mind a spring campaign that I might not want to miss. However, I had my way about it and he gave me letters of introduction to prominent officials in Washington, and I departed.

The ice had gone out of the Yellowstone, and a small party of non-commissioned officers and soldiers was about to start on some business down the river in a large boat, or mackinaw, so I made shift to secure passage and I make no doubt but I paid my way in steering that old tub through perilous rapids and around the rocks and snags. I have a letter before me, written a few years ago by one of the soldiers, Mr. L. Barker, now of Clay Center, Kansas. "I have always held you in grateful remembrance since we made that voyage down the Yellowstone," he writes. "That ride through the ice and uprooted treetops worried me more than all the Indian fighting I ever did."

Turning a bend near the mouth of the river, we came

GENERAL NELSON A. MILES IN 1877

suddenly upon an ice jam extending high above the banks that blocked the channel from side to side and we made haste to reach the shore. In the night the ice gorge broke with much grinding and din, leaving a solid wall on each side of the channel, and next morning, after a survey to see if old *Minnishushu* was clear, we made our way through this forbidding avenue of thrashing water until the broad and swollen current of the Missouri received our battered craft and wafted us along a wooded bend for the space of a mile to a plain on the farther bank, where stood the military post of Fort Buford.

My stay in the East was short. City life, though exciting enough, was not to my liking, and aside from the pleasure of a reunion with the home folks and meeting again the friends of my boyhood, a trip to New York and Washington completed the rounds and I was ready to return to the plains and mountains of Montana and Dakota.

I had my own saddle and in Bismarck, Dakota Territory, I borrowed a pony and set out for the lonely ride up the Missouri. Of this journey I have little recollection until I reached a cabin halfway between Fort Berthold and the mouth of the Yellowstone. Here the hunter who occupied the cabin informed me that an Indian bound for the Yellowstone had camped there the previous night and was not more than three hours ahead of me. I was now on familiar ground, though I had last traveled the trail almost ten years before, when I had my first serious conflict with wild Indians. I had been on the trail about two hours when I suddenly came upon a mounted Indian. I recognized him at once as Two Moons, one of the chiefs who had fought us at Wolf

Mountain the previous winter. We shook hands and proceeded on our way in perfect amity.

Two Moons was the leader of one of the bands of Cheyenne and Sioux that came in and submitted to General Miles in preference to going to the southern agencies to surrender, as many of the Indians did. He was on his way back from the Middle West, whither he had gone with other leading men to visit General Sheridan at his headquarters in Chicago, on some mission, as I understood him, for the establishment of his people in or near the Yellowstone Valley. A few months before this, in bitter cold, we had been pursuing and fighting these Indians, who were about the wildest and fiercest on the plains. Now, in good fellowship, Two Moons and I rode along the trail, single file as though we had always been the best of friends.

Two Moons weighed about two hundred pounds and had a pleasant face. He wore a black felt hat with a feather and garnished band, a woolen shirt, leggings, moccasins, and a painted robe adorned with picture writing. If he carried a revolver it was not in evidence. At the crossing of the Yellowstone he spied a wildcat high in a cottonwood tree and called my attention to it by pointing upward. I stopped and saw the animal on the topmost bough. I drew a bead on him and he fell almost at our feet, to the great satisfaction of my companion, who exclaimed, *Ah-hi! waste!* or something to this effect, as though it was something of a feat. I skinned the beast and gave the pelt to him, which seemed to please him greatly.

By easy stages we made Tongue River, our destination. On this journey along the Yellowstone I noted the scarcity of game, though it was not the season when it

A Winter Pursuit

might be found in abundance along a line of travel. Two Moons, noticing my sweep of the plain for some moving object, shook his head and said, "No buffaloes," and pointing to the road, "Plenty wagon tracks, buffaloes take to high ground." And it was true that on the hills beyond the valley buffaloes were grazing.

CHAPTER XI

CHIEF JOSEPH COMES TO THE END OF THE TRAIL

EARLY in the spring of 1877 I was directed to go north to the Missouri River and beyond to look for hostile Indians that had escaped north to the border in the previous year. Sitting Bull and his band had barely missed capture on the Red Water when Lieutenant Frank D. Baldwin with a detachment of infantry charged the camp in a snowstorm. Joe Culbertson, a fine type of frontiersman, was guide on this occasion and did excellent work here and elsewhere. The Indians got away, but they lost a lot of equipage and some horses.

I well remember the night that Lieutenant Baldwin returned to the cantonment on Tongue River and made his report. I was with General Miles in his tent-covered hut, having called on him in the evening, and he was relating some adventure of the battle of Chancellorsville when a tap on the door was followed by the entrance of this staff officer fresh from the field, who was greeted warmly by the General. After shaking hands, I excused myself and retired for I saw that they had much to talk about.

For my trip north I selected to accompany me Red Mike, who was now a scout, and Haddo, a young corporal of the Fifth Infantry, who made one or two trips with me and was a fine fellow as well as a good shot. He was killed in the fight at the Bear Paw Mountains when Chief Joseph of the Nez Percés surrendered. I did not know that Haddo was a medal of honor man until I saw it in a book published almost thirty years later.

The region of country between the mouth of Tongue River on the Yellowstone and Big Dry Creek had become familiar ground since I first traversed it with Vic Smith in the late fall of 1876. Then we had traveled in the night for safety; now we three were traveling at our leisure in broad daylight with no pressing anxiety, for were we not free scouts? Anyway, it was at least two sleeps to the nearest camp of hostile Indians.

Though we had meat on the pack Mike shot an antelope and we camped in a coulee near an old gnarled cottonwood, close to a water-hole. I remember that roasting bones of the antelope kept us busy far into the night —a treat in a safe camp before rolling into our blankets. A most appetizing odor arises from bones roasting before an open fire, an odor that promotes congeniality and fires expectation.

After we had crossed the Missouri and were jogging along a grassy plain covered with a new fall of snow, Haddo looked behind and shouted, "Look back!" We stopped, and turning saw a bunch of buffalo bulls, twenty or more, headed for us at full speed, driven by five Indians.

We dismounted and stood to one side, watching to see what would happen. Before the animals came abreast of us they swerved a little and one Indian, lunging alongside one of the buffaloes, deftly let loose two arrows that buried themselves in his shaggy hide. His example was followed by two others of the racing riders. One of them, an elderly man, stopped his horse beside us and dismounted. Letting his pony stand, he reached for a buck-skin pipe sack, and holding it up said: *Cha-*

shasha, ota; chanda, no; which meant "Red willow plenty, tobacco none."

"Who are you?" I demanded.

He replied, "Yanktoni mea."

I felt for a piece of plug that I carried especially for this purpose, and gave it to him. His face lighted up, and gathering his robe around him he rose easily to the homemade saddle, the seat of which was covered with a strip of calf-skin. Before he started after his companions he told us that they were killing buffaloes with arrows because they were short of powder and cartridges, which they were saving for deer and elk. "Tonight," he said, "plenty of buffalo meat, plenty of smoke."

His companions had already disappeared from view, but they left their sign along the trail in the shape of dead buffaloes. At one carcass which we passed there was a quirt or riding whip across the neck to indicate ownership. It looked as though there might be other Indians coming along to skin these animals, and we made haste to get along before they should arrive.

I do not remember just how or when Good Dog, a Yankton whom I had known several years, came to us and stuck—a self-appointed escort or guardian—but it must have been near old Fort Peck, after swinging around from the Milk River country, that we ran into a bunch of Indians, men, women, and children, with travois, returning from trade at Fort Peck and now looking for a convenient camping ground. Three Indians that spied us came dashing up from the far side of the ravine and as soon as they were out of sight in the hollow we swerved to the right to cross lower down. The Indians seemed to be animated by the same purpose, for when we reached the crest of ground that gave to the hollow and could look over a little the heads of the three bobbed up directly in front of us. They quickly vanished, however, and we saw them no more.

Good Dog was near by and seemed concerned. To our questions he replied rather evasively that they came from beyond the Milk River. I learned later on that these people were from the bands that had joined Sitting Bull at Woody Mountain, across the line. It was easy to see why these Indians, enjoying the protection of the English government north of the boundary, ranged south of the line where hunting was easy and game abundant in the lower Milk River country, while the terms of barter were more favorable at the Missouri River posts than at Woody Mountain, and the young men could engage in a raid or two and then skip back to the North.

After two days' travel, during which we circled around the lower Milk River country, encountering only a friendly camp of Assiniboin, we turned our horses again in the direction of the Missouri. We learned from these friendly Indians that one of their young men had seen a large village of the Sioux from Woody Mountain camped on Frenchman's Creek early in the spring, and that they were killing many buffaloes, which accounted for the numerous herds that drifted down the valley of Milk River soon after. They also had made a killing, and every lodge had fresh and dried meat.

On our return we found the Big Dry, which usually carries only a dribble of water, channel-full from bank to bank. It looked bad, but we selected a crossing where the water barely came to the bellies of our horses. In some way Mike's horse stumbled in midstream, and in order to save the animal from falling Mike jumped off, and before the horse recovered his footing Mike's rifle slipped from the leather case attached to the side of his saddle and was washed away. We searched some time for the gun, by trying to feel for it with our feet, but had no success. It was a serious loss and Haddo, who stood guard while Mike and I waded across and up stream, loaned him his revolver. We stopped where wood was handy, built a fire, and dried the only clothes we possessed, while Mike vowed that he would come back when the water was out and hunt for his rifle.

Early in the summer I made another trip across country to the Missouri, and again and again as the Nez Percé trouble culminated in a retreat before General Howard's forces in Idaho to the district of the Yellowstone. On one of these trips I was accompanied by John Howard. He was an Englishman of versatile understanding, who had seen much of the world, and having worn the edge off military life in the Old World, now sought diversion in a new field of action. He was a cheerful companion and talked entertainingly on many subjects. If he is still on "this poor ledge" I trust that he will recall when our tea gave out and we brewed tea from wild cherry bark, in a region where there is no good water to drink. Memory affords but vague details of this trip, though I remember that at the crossing far above Fort Peck we found a broad river, and stripping our horses, drove them naked into the river and urged them to the farther shore; then, placing saddles, bridles, guns, and clothing on a flimsy raft, we pushed it ahead of us as we swam the stream.

I was kept on the move all these summer months. On one occasion I made a trip to Carroll, when I saw my old acquaintance, Major Reed, again, and a steamboat unloading government ammunition. I was with a party of four or five men, all civilians, and we passed down Lodge Pole Creek to a pleasant camp in a nest of dry cottonwoods with grass all around. We had several buffalo tongues and some hump ribs. One of the party was expert at cooking buffalo humps. An excavation was made for the fire, and the hump ribs were prepared with pepper and salt and what other condiment, paste, or relish, I will not say (it being the cook's secret) but when the fire-hole was aglow with live coals the hump, in a piece of green hide, was consigned to it, the mass of coals was drawn over it, and over all dry earth was packed. When the hole was opened in the morning and the skin cover removed the steaming hump was revealed, juicy and brown, cooked to a turn. At least we thought so, as seated around the camp fire with tin cups filled with coffee we attacked this choice roast. It was a feast to make one wish for absent friends to be present and enjoy.

As we broke camp and approached the Musselshell, which was close by, a string of Indians was seen coming afoot through the edge of the timber at right angles to our course. They did not seem to be alarmed by our approach, and we awaited them at the edge of the timber. They traveled, as usual, in single file, twelve or fifteen in number, and halted, leaning on their rifles, while the leader came to us. They were Sioux from the north, returning home after a raid for Crow horses. They did not have much to say, nor did they tarry. Uncommunicative, but not unfriendly, they passed along and I noted that they were clad in Hudson's Bay blankets and head-cloths of a somber color.

I made another trip to Carroll about the time the

Nez Percés, whom General Howard was pursuing, slipped around the Seventh Cavalry near Heart Mountain and headed for the Judith Basin. General Miles ordered me to accompany Lieutenant Bailey of the Fifth Infantry and a detachment of cavalry to Carroll to forestall any attempt the Nez Percés might make to raid the ammunition stored there. We rode by easy stages across the Big Dry to the Musselshell a few miles above its junction with the Missouri. Crossing the Musselshell near the place where we had encountered the Indians on the occasion of my last journey to Carroll, I led the detachment to Crooked Creek, as it is now called, and across to the long ridge that looks down upon the Missouri, where the wild Indians may have looked down in wonder at the boats of Lewis and Clark as they ascended the stream two generations earlier.

At midday we saw below us the houses and cabins of Carroll, the descent to which was long and slow. We found the government ammunition locked in a small building and apparently no one responsible for it, but soon Major Reed came along and we learned that he had kept an eye on the property, and had caused it to be locked up. He could give us no information about the Nez Percés, but late in the day came Bill Norris with a message from General Miles directing me to join the command at the mouth of the Musselshell. I was surprised to learn that the General and his troops were at the Musselshell, for when we left the cantonment on the Yellowstone there was no movement on foot for an expedition. I saddled my horse and wended my way along the ridges, disturbing much game in the evening time. There was little air stirring and I remember that a mountain lion crossed my path, tempting me to take a shot at him. As the darkness fell the sky became luminous with stars, and it was still and warm on the high ground. When I had descended at midnight I came into the chill air of the lowlands, and found and followed the fresh trail of the column leading down the Musselshell.

Presently I saw the dying light of a camp fire and soon came to where the pack train had unloaded with its rows of *aparejos.* I stopped at the fire long enough to swallow a cup of hot coffee and to inquire of the watchman as to the location of headquarters. Learning that General Miles was aboard the steamboat at the river's bank, half a mile away, I traveled on through camps of sleeping soldiers, unchallenged, to the steamer, and found General Miles and his aide, Captain Baldwin, the only people about, engaged in a friendly tussle to determine which should have first choice of two beds that had been spread on the deck for them. They laughed when they saw me coming, and the General told me that he intended to cross the river soon and wanted me to take the scouts and go ahead and pick up the Nez Percé trail if it could be found, though the Nez Percés were last reported in the Judith Basin.

I retired and went to sleep somewhere. It was now past one o'clock A.M., September 25, 1877. In the morning I learned that some troops had been put across the river the day before to scout the country and that the General was waiting for news. At any rate he allowed the steamer to go, but it was still in sight when a couple of men came down the river in a small boat and said that the Nez Percés had crossed below Cow Island, forty or fifty miles above.

The steamer was almost out of sight when General Miles ordered a field gun to be fired with shell, and jumping onto a stump he waved an army blanket to attract attention. The people on the boat evidently heard the gun or saw the shell explode along the bluffs, for it presently came back and the scouts crossed on the first trip.

We rode rapidly a general course northwest, about thirty or thirty-five miles to the group of Little Rocky Mountains, and ascending a prominent peak near the eastern end, searched the country beyond with our glasses. Below our point of observation lay People's Creek, its course being traced a long way in the direction of Milk River. Beyond People's Creek to the left extended a broken plain to the foot of the Bear Paw Mountains, hazy and dim in the distance. From the Bear Paw to the Missouri every ridge was scrutinized for signs of travelers, for it was apparent that no great company of people with a multitude of live stock could conceal from view their movement on that open plain, nor would they try, expecting pursuit only from the rear. We looked long and earnestly, but no object appeared to move, not even buffaloes where one might expect plenty.

The day was advancing and light was failing. Nothing could be seen of the command, but the view of the country to the east was obstructed by buttes and ridges. We descended from the lookout which gave such an excellent view of the region the Nez Percés would have to cross to reach the boundary line to John Bull's country. I reasoned that the Indians, having put the Missouri between them and their pursuers, might rest near the river for a day at least before renewing their march. On the other hand, if they had passed on without halting we would pick up the trail by striking across to the foot of the Bear Paw. Before doing this I wanted to ascertain General Miles' course after leaving the end of the Little Rocky Mountains, at the east end of which, I surmised, he would camp that night. So we pushed along the foothills until we struck his trail, and following it for a mile or two found the command in camp.

The camp, made just as they halted on rough ground, had more the appearance of a bivouac, though as evening was near I could not see much of it. There were some Sioux and Cheyenne present, organized from the surrounding Indians as an auxiliary force. I had not seen them as yet and I surmised that they were camping by themselves.

On reporting the result of my observations to the General, he directed me, as I had expected, to push on in search of the trail. I at once set about hunting up scouts and selected three: Haddo, my soldier scout, Milan Tripp, and one other. Tripp was a new man. Someone whose opinion I respected brought him to me and said: "Milan is employed to drive some beef cattle in order to give him a job, but he will give better service as a scout if you can arrange it."

We started without delay for I wished to get clear of the camp while it was still daylight, for the weather looked threatening, with signs of rain. We had not gone very far before we were overhauled by Lieutenant Maus, a gallant young officer whom I did not know, but of whom I had heard good accounts. He had two soldiers with him, but the equipment of all three was such that they would scarcely be taken on the prairie for soldiers, a desirable thing in itself, for if we ran into the Nez Percés they would hardly suspect that we were connected with a military command. Lieutenant Maus now assumed command of the party, but we proceeded as before.

It soon became too dark to distinguish objects near by or any trails that we might pass, and the air was misty with moisture. Under the circumstances I suggested to Lieutenant Maus that we halt where we were until it should become light enough to see our way, there being some rough ground ahead. Near some grass we unsaddled and let our stock nibble the short buffalo grass. The air was perfectly still, as is usually the case in a stiff mist that carries fine rain. After a while we secured our horses and each disposed himself as best he could to rest until the pall should be lifted, or dawn of day should make it possible to proceed on our quest.

As for myself, I placed the narrow folds of my saddle blanket against the saddle on a smooth spot, and wrapping the blanket that I carried as a roll in place of a coat about me, I lay down and tried to sleep, but could not for thinking of the necessity of being on the way at first light. However, I did sleep, for hours afterward Haddo awakened me, saying that the mist was lifting and morning near.

All were roused and the horses were saddled. It appeared to be a retired spot and we undertook to light a fire and make some coffee, but before this was accomplished the head of the column appeared in sight some distance off and we mounted and sped off for fear that the troops would get ahead of us. I do not remember how far we had advanced before the light of day made clear the view ahead, but our course led to a gap in the Bear Paw Mountains directly in front of us. The clear air made beautiful the mountains, partly shrouded in clouds and mist that wasted slowly under the rays of the morning sun. As we rode now at a trot or canter across the pebbly mesas approaching the foothills of the Bear Paw, I noted for the first time the singular line of rock monuments, or tall cones, that occur at regular intervals along their face.

Suddenly as we were mounting a rise of ground that commanded a view of the country to our left I saw some objects afar off moving toward the base of the mountain. We halted, and observing them through our glasses, made out two horsemen driving some ponies. Presently they disappeared into a narrow valley that ran along the base of the mountain and we hurried on to intercept them. They must have heard us pounding the turf for when we came to the edge of the hill looking down into the hollow they had stopped and were listening, or seemed to be.

They now abandoned their horses and ran up the rocky hillside, where there was cover of brush which concealed them from view. It was impossible to descend into the valley at this point and before a trail was found the Indians were halfway up the mountain. Some of the scouts, however, did not wait for orders, but commenced shooting. Simultaneously with the first report of the rifles the discovery was made that the broad Nez Percé trail lay before us in the hollow, and the recently abandoned camping ground, with the remains of several buffalo carcasses scattered around.

The scouts were ordered to stop firing, for it was not a part of our business to pursue these Indians, who were now on the trail and near the gap. We descended to the abandoned camp-ground and noted that one trail led over the mountain through the pass, but whether this was the main trail it was impossible to tell at once as the

Nez Percés had such a multitude of horses that all other trails were obliterated. Lieutenant Maus sent a dispatch to General Miles apprising him of our discovery and Milan Tripp, having the best mount, was selected to carry it. There was now nothing to do but await the approach of the troops.

General Miles was quick to take advantage of the slightest incident to further success. A change in the weather hid his command from observation, and led by his Sioux and Cheyenne Indians he advanced through the mist to the right point of the Bear Paw, where he stood ready to surprise the Nez Percés in their camp or to intercept them on their march north to the Canadian border.

We waited some time for the arrival of the command, when, suspecting that General Miles had moved to the eastward of our position, I suggested to Lieutenant Maus that we move along the base of the mountain and get in touch with the column. We had gone but a short distance when we came upon a broad, fresh trail, which showed that the troops had passed and were about a mile ahead.

We pushed on more rapidly, but before we overtook the command it had struck the Nez Percé camp. The first charge and dash had given way to an investment, a cordon of troops being drawn around the entrenched position of the Indians, for true to the lesson implanted in the battle of the Big Hole it was the practice of these Indians, thereafter, to entrench or build defenses at every important camp. Looking down into the hollow, I could see nothing but a few skin lodges. The women and children were safely secreted in underground excavations, while the warriors held a number of well-

CHIEF JOSEPH, NEZ PERCÉ

Courtesy Museum of the American Indian.

placed rock rifle pits, from whose shelter they picked off any who showed their heads.

Joseph and his followers were trapped at last, and excepting the fieldpiece that occasionally mouthed a shell into the seemingly deserted hollow the battle had degenerated into a duel between sharpshooters on either side. I noted that the troops were disposed in such a way as to inclose the hollow that concealed the Nez Percés and prevent their escape.

The ground about the place was bare of timber, and I unsaddled my horse near where the pack train had camped, just below the fieldpiece, which was vomiting shot at intervals into the center of the Indian stronghold. There was no excitement, and I remember seeing Lieutenant Baird of the staff go by with a bullet-hole through one of his ears, while Captain Carter was talking earnestly to General Miles. The Captain's company had met a murderous fire when it charged the camp and the men had been forced to hug the ground for some time before they could return the fire and force the Indians to take cover. The cavalry had suffered, also, and two gallant officers and a number of brave troopers were killed in the first dash. Behind the first line I saw a row of bodies covered with blankets.

I saw an Indian named Hump, a bold and picturesque fellow, crawling along the ground toward a rifle pit that held a warrior who had taken heavy toll of the soldiers. I watched Hump as he wormed his way skilfully from one little depression to another. He could travel flat on the ground with the greatest ease, but I did not envy him his present quest. Another Indian had started with him, perhaps to give him encouragement and support, but he had stopped halfway and from his vantage point, which was as close to mother earth as an Indian could get, lay watching Hump's farther advance.

Others were watching too, as well as myself, among them several Sioux and Cheyenne scouts, who were friends of Hump. Suddenly Hump came to a stop, and shifting his position slightly, pulled his rifle slowly to the front and carefully sighted it toward an object at an angle to his line of advance. He fired, gazed a moment, then crooned a war-note which was heard by his waiting friends, and edged along on the course he had pursued. He had killed his man, for when the Nez Percés surrendered we found a rifle pit in the direction of his fire, and in it, cold and stiff, a warrior bowed over his rifle.

It would have been better if Hump had retreated after the shot, which he could have done with honor, having counted a coup, for he had progressed but a little way when he sensed his enemy, who was having his hands full just then with other opponents all along the line. The course Hump had pursued was down a grassy draw that led to a certain point where it was commanded by two or three rifle pits and would be under an enfilading fire.

Finally, still hugging the ground closely, Hump came in sight of the ragged tips of the rock pile which sheltered the warrior who, so far immune, had with matchless skill and desperate courage countered every attempt to dislodge him. Several of our men had tried conclusions with him from various nooks, but one had been killed outright and two more were disabled and under the surgeon's care. For the moment, apparently, the warrior's attention was directed elsewhere, and I could see by Hump's attitude that he was waiting for some sign before placing a shot.

Chief Joseph's Retreat

Finally it came, and raising himself slightly Hump fired twice quickly, but his opponents were not idle, for he himself received a bullet that laid him flat on the ground for several minutes. We thought for a moment that he was dead, but he was only motionless, trying to locate the new enemy. He gave it up, however, and satisfied, perhaps, that he had counted all the coups possible, painfully worked his way back to his friend, who assisted him to safety.

I wandered along the line and came upon Corporal Haddo, who had borrowed my field glasses and was trying to locate the Nez Percé who was working such havoc among the soldiers. I told him to be careful about exposing his head over the crest, but I very soon became interested in this fellow who was exchanging shots with sharpshooters at other points, and told Haddo to place the glasses on a roll of his coat, and keeping as low as possible, mark the hole in the rock from which the Indian fired, and I would try to get him. He soon indicated the spot and I fired at it twice, with what result I cannot say, but I do not think the distance was over a hundred yards.

I now left him to seek the camp of the packers, for I wanted a cup of coffee and some meat. Before going I advised Haddo not to stay in one place but to move along and keep low. He said that he wanted one more shot and then he would hunt the company and see what they had to eat. While I was eating my lunch at the pack train someone came and said that Haddo had been shot just above the heart. I ran to the place and found him speechless and dying, Poor Haddo! a fine man and a good soldier. I missed him much. Cool and fearless, he had been my companion on many trips.

"Yellowstone Kelly"

That night, September 30, was dark and lowering, which increased the difficulties of the extra pickets stationed to prevent the Nez Percés from escaping. I spread my blankets near the headquarters bivouac in a hollow filled with sleeping men, and lay awake, listening to the intermittent firing as individual Nez Percés sought to escape between the lines under cover of the darkness. Finally, I fell asleep, but later in the night I was awakened by someone calling my name. It was an order from headquarters to proceed on the back trail to meet and bring in a wagon train that was following the command.

I rose and called another scout and together we hunted our horses. On reaching the battle field that morning I had left my horse saddled, thinking I might need him, but later on had removed the saddle and bridle, which I left with the pack train, letting my horse feed while there was still grass to be had. I had not seen him since. I felt that it was useless to hunt for him on a night like this, so we went down to one of the cavalry camps, for I knew that the cavalry had spare horses after the day's fight, and procuring a couple of mounts, we started off in the gloom of a starless night.

I had no information as to the probable whereabouts of the train, but I assumed that it had followed the command the day before and had been delayed by the necessity of cutting down banks and making fills. I was satisfied that as soon as night struck the men would go into camp, and as soon as camp was made a fire would be made unless an officer was along to forbid it. We lost the trail many times in the darkness, and finally left it for good, relying on some glimmer of firelight to guide us. We proceeded as far as the crossing of People's

Creek, when I called a halt, feeling that we had passed the train in the darkness. I was not worried for I knew that the men could not travel after darkness set in, and that they would push on with the first flush of dawn.

The sequel confirmed my conjectures. At first dawn of day I took our bearings and we were soon following the wagon tracks. We would have overtaken the train before it reached the camp where the Nez Percés were being held at bay, had I not seen off at the right a lot of horses on a sidehill which I thought it important to investigate. On the battle field there were rumors that Sitting Bull with a large force of Sioux was near the boundary line ready to render assistance to the battling Nez Percés. We turned abruptly off our course, sought cover, and gradually approached the horses, which were feeding quietly on a hillside and in the gulch beyond. Riding among them, I found that they were nearly all branded U.S., and I was satisfied that they belonged to the command.

As the camp was not over two miles away I decided to leave the animals where they were for the present, and speeding along on our way, we found that the wagon train had arrived safely. Reporting the matter of the government horses so far away from camp without a guard, General Miles informed me that a lot of stock had stampeded in the night. Much concern was felt lest they had fallen into the hands of predatory bands of Sioux, and parties had been sent out to trace them. His own saddle horse, a very valuable animal, was among them. By his direction I took another scout and returned to the place where I had discovered the stock, and rounding up more than a hundred horses, mules, and ponies, returned safely with them to camp.

"Yellowstone Kelly"

It was on this day, as I remember, that Chief Joseph asked for a parley, and Lieutenant Jerome of the cavalry went into the Nez Percé camp as a pledge, I think; anyway, he was detained, and after his release told of being held in an underground passage the Indians had excavated, a damp and chilly place where the warriors danced to keep warm, and finally left him, saying, "We must fight again pretty soon to get warm."

On the fourth of October came General Howard with a small escort. I remember seeing him and General Miles seated on the grass in consultation, with the other officers grouped near by. On the following morning Chief Joseph surrendered to General Miles.

That day or the next, after the dead had been buried, the camp was moved a short distance to where a little valley gave out from the mountain, and here travois were constructed for the wounded and other preparations made for the long trip to the Yellowstone. General Miles says in his account of that date: "Our wounded suffered greatly, owing to the rough broken country passed over, and some died en route. On reaching the Missouri, I found two steamers that had come up from Fort Buford in response to my dispatch of September 17, and these furnished supplies and food, and upon them I placed all the severely wounded soldiers and Indians, sent them down to the nearest hospital, and with the remainder we moved across the country to the Yellowstone. The command looked like a great caravan moving over the prairie—the troops, a large herd of captured stock, prisoners, ambulances, and pack and wagon trains, all covered by an advance guard, flankers, and rear guard."

CHAPTER XII

NORTHWARD TO THE CANADIAN BORDER

I WAS not with the command on that journey, for just before breaking camp General Miles sent for me and said, "I want you to go north with dispatches for General Terry, who is now on his way from Fort Benton to meet the British commissioners on the boundary line." I had not known before of the joint commission to establish the status of Sitting Bull and other hostiles, who in great numbers had fled across the border. The General handed me a large official envelope which I did not for a moment know what to do with as I had no pocket large enough for it, but I stuck it in my belt and said, "General, I will take one of the scouts with me in case I should need a man." I picked Tom Newcomb, who had joined the scouts a few days before from somewhere, and was noticeable on this occasion as he had on leggings made of red blanket stuff.

We lost no time in getting started on our journey and wound along the west end of the Bear Paw Mountains as the troops moved south. On the other side of Crow Creek we met a lone horseman on the trail, leading a fine horse. To my query as to the whereabouts of General Terry the man said: "General Terry left Fort Benton yesterday, and will camp at ——— Spring tonight. When you get around the point of the Bear Paw, strike due north and you will hit their camp."

When we got around the spur of the mountain I laid a course due north and we traveled on over a rolling prairie all the afternoon. About dusk we saw a light straight ahead which seemed near but was afar, for we traveled hours before it loomed as a camp fire, in whose light we passed around a considerable camp of infantry and cavalry to a group of tents, where we dismounted and asked the guard if General Terry occupied the large tent. The guard replying in the affirmative, I tapped and entered, Tom Newcomb following.

The tent seemed a very large one, even for a headquarters, and was comfortably furnished. I recognized General Terry, whom I had seen before, and an officer coming forward, I stated that I had dispatches from General Miles and gave them to him. The General, who was seated, came toward us and questioned me concerning the campaign just ended, and learning that we had left the command that morning he directed a young officer to find us refreshment and a place to sleep.

The officer went in search of a sergeant, who came and showed us a tent that we could occupy for the night. He gave us grain for our horses and we unsaddled and fed them on the spot. Then he piloted us to a company mess tent, where we filled up on hard-tack, bacon, beans, and cold coffee. The pangs of hunger having succumbed to the ordeal, we wandered back to the A tent, for we now had a vast desire for sleep after our hard day's ride. With our saddles for pillows, I held a lighted match while Newcomb spread the blankets, or as he facetiously termed them, "wind-tanglers," on the coarse but comfortable straw mattress, and I remember nothing more than the remark of my companion, "This beats camping out."

In the morning at the bugle call for reveille I arose and looked about me on a familiar camp scene that was full of life. A company of infantrymen near by were engaged in various duties. Some were rolling their blankets into suitable bundles to place on the wagons; others had their haversacks and were waiting the call for breakfast. The tents, if they had any, had already been disposed of. Farther on troopers were returning from water and were rubbing down their mounts at the horse line. I cannot remember now the strength of this military force that formed the escort to General Terry, but I think there were two troops of the Second Cavalry and one or two companies of the Seventh Infantry. To carry all their impedimenta required a number of heavy wagons, and there they were, the old U.S. army wagons with wooden boxes painted blue, with six mules tied to each one and the drivers putting on the harness.

Breakfast call sounded—most inspiring note—and I called Newcomb, for I saw the sergeant beckoning me to the mess tent. While Newcomb was getting ready I walked down to the watering place and scrubbed my hands and face as well as I could. After breakfast with the company, I noted that the officers were in no hurry to break camp, and looking around for my horse, saw that he had been fed. I do not remember the names of any of the officers with whom I had conversation, but before the march began General Terry sent for me and said, "Kelly, I want you to carry a letter to the line, where you will meet the English commission or their representative, to whom you will deliver the letter and return with the answer."

We took the road, Newcomb and I, over the same rolling country, but I remember some dry lakes on one side of Milk River and many, many antelopes, beautiful creatures! After we made the crossing of Milk River we fell in with three young Sioux Indians, well armed, who appeared suddenly as if from nowhere. They sat on their horses regarding us.

"Where are the *Sagadashas?*" I inquired.

They pointed to the hills to the right of the road. These Indians have a habit of gesturing with their mouth to indicate direction or an object that may be seen, and such a gesture was made by one of these young men. I laid my field glasses in the direction indicated and saw a lone horseman on a hill and on either side of him, at an interval of a mile or so, two elevations that I recognized as mounds marking the international boundary.

We followed the road a while, then turned off directly toward the lone horseman. As I had suspected, he proved to be a vidette who had been posted to give information of the approach of the Americans. His uniform indicated that he was a member of the Northwest Mounted Police. He informed me that his party was in camp a short distance away, and we proceeded until we came to a conical wall tent, differing somewhat from our Sibley tent of that day. Near by was a light wagon, and beside it a light tent fly was pitched, sheltering three men, one of them an officer. He courteously welcomed us and I delivered the letter to him.

The camp had been pitched near a spring and, with grass all about it, was a pleasant enough place. The simplicity of equipment and the absence of military pomp was in marked contrast to the imposing establishment maintained by General Terry. The hero of Fort Fisher believed in traveling in comfort as well as in state. And why not, when you have the command and the opportunity? Troops grow rusty in quarters and their upkeep costs but little more in the field than when housed in post or cantonment. Soldiers are not averse to camp life, especially in pleasant weather.

In the morning we left our agreeable hosts and turned our horses in the direction from which we had come, to meet General Terry's command which was traveling the same road. The English people broke camp for the same purpose. On rejoining the command I presented my letter to General Terry, who shortly afterward went into camp near White Horse Lake, and here the English party joined us.

Early the next morning the General took the road with a small following, leaving all the troops and nearly all the transportation in camp. It was said that Sitting Bull, upon hearing through his spies of the approach of a formidable American force, told the English officers that he would not attend any council if soldiers were present, and if the American officer wanted to hold a council with the Indians he must leave his soldiers at the border.

With Newcomb I followed the commission, and when we had nearly caught up with it the quartermaster, Captain Freeman, I think, rode up and said, "Did you not understand that no one was to cross the border except those whom General Terry had specially indicated?"

"No," I replied, "I supposed that we were to proceed with the party and return with dispatches."

"No," said the quartermaster, "the order is plain; you must return to the camp." And without further ado he turned his horse and regained his party, while we stood in the road looking at one another. I was much disappointed and not fully satisfied that the quartermaster was correct in his understanding of the orders, or in his zeal in applying them. There were bound to be some hot speeches at the council, and I wanted much to be present and observe the situation. Though General Miles had made no suggestion that I pursue my journey to the place set for the council, I felt that he would not be displeased if I gleaned at first hand any information of interest that would be of value to his command.

We returned to the camp by the Lake of the Milky Water. I do not remember how many days we waited here for the return of the party from the north, but I was glad to turn my face southward once more and leave these cheerless plains, which had charmed me in former years when they were thronged with buffaloes and antelopes, and elk in great bands were found along the wooded streams and mountain slopes near by. Now the elk had wandered or been frightened away by the many bands of hostile Indians camped along the border, whose hunting parties had cleared the plains of buffaloes.

We headed for the east end of the Bear Paw Mountains, thinking to pass over the Nez Percé battle ground, which we had not gone over thoroughly at the time of the surrender. We had almost reached the place when we were suddenly surrounded by a band of twelve or fifteen Indians. We were taken completely by surprise, for our attention had been concentrated on the prospect of game, but with our rifles in our hands we were equal to the occasion.

As they made no hostile movement I made the usual sign, asking who they were. They answered by a sign that I did not understand. Newcomb, who had been in the lower country, said at once on hearing them talk, that they were Pawnee, but I knew that the Pawnee did not come so far north, and then it dawned on me that they were prairie Grosventres. I asked them in the sign language if they were prairie Big Bellies; they nodded their heads and shouted, "Aye," but some only grunted and laughed at my grotesque attempt at the sign name. They were fine-looking fellows and were well armed. I noticed they had some brass-mounted Henry rifles and double-barrel shotguns for running buffaloes. They told me they had unearthed a cache made by the Nez Percés, and that they had seen the smoke of a steamer on the river. They soon went their way and we pursued ours.

The battle field, forsaken of life, looked gruesome enough with its scattered bones of cavalry horses and mounds of freshly piled earth that covered the remains of soldiers and warriors who had answered their last roll-call. The cache which the prairie Indians had discovered exposed a gaping hole in the ground filled with miscellaneous goods and household effects, all new, as though they had just been removed from a warehouse. Cooking utensils of all kinds, pillows, clothing, and other articles were mingled in the utmost confusion, while flour, sugar, and other provisions were scattered over the ground. When the Nez Percés crossed the Missouri near Cow Island they had captured a lot of freight that a steamboat had unloaded on the bank, and this explained the cache and its contents.

We took the trail for the Missouri and at nightfall went into camp. In the morning we found three horses on the trail, one of which proved to be General Miles' saddle horse, a beautiful white animal, which had been lost in a stampede on the first night of the investment of the Nez Percés. Separated from the mass of flying animals, the white horse had consorted with two Indian ponies and through instinct had gradually worked around to the trail over which he entered the country.

I shifted my saddle and equipment to the General's horse, after which we resumed our way, driving the loose animals before us. When we drew near the valley of the Missouri we met two white men driving a bunch of ponies along the trail. They seemed to be in a hurry, but paused long enough to inform us that there was a steamboat at the river and three troops of the Seventh Cavalry in camp. Urging our horses forward, we soon entered the open cottonwood timber of the Missouri bottom and came to where the cavalry were in camp alongside a river steamer. One of General Miles' aides was aboard, and I turned over the General's horse to him. Captain Benteen of the Seventh was in command of the three troops of cavalry, and after I had had some conversation with him the boat ferried us across the river, there being no ford in the vicinity. The remainder of our journey to the cantonment lay over familiar ground and nothing worthy of note was experienced.

The Nez Percés were scarcely settled in comfortable camps near the cantonment when orders were received from Washington to send them down the river. Under military guard they were taken overland to Bismarck, and eventually to Indian Territory, where half of them soon died of malarial fever. Quiet reigned in the valley of the Yellowstone, and soon settlers began coming into the country to establish homes and subdue the wilderness. I was ordered to make a trip to Deadwood in the Black Hills to determine the feasibility of a wagon route to the mouth of the Tongue River on the Yellowstone, with the idea of establishing a mail line, this being

Northward to the Border

a shorter route than the one by way of Bismarck and Fort Buford. The original order, written in ink that is still unfaded, is before me:

Capt. Heintzelman, P.Q.M.
Sir: The commanding officer of this post has issued an order to equip a small detail to accompany L. S. Kelly on D.S. The wagon brought in by Cris Gilson is to be used and the C.O. directs that two of your stoutest horses be used with the wagon.

> Respectfully,
> G. W. Baird, Adjt. & A.A.A.G.

April 25, 1878.

Headquarters, District of the Yellowstone.

> Fort Keogh, Montana Territory
> April 26, 1878.

This detachment of four men is sent out from these headquarters to examine the country between this place and the Black Hills. All officers of this command are directed, and all others requested, to render to them any needed assistance.

> N. A. Miles, Col. Fifth Infantry.
> Bvt. Brig. General, U.S.A.

My intention was to travel across country where a wagon trail would be found only occasionally, hence the light wagon, which appeared to be a modified buckboard, admirably adapted to buck the rivers, coulees, and ravines en route. The detail consisted of Sergeant Gilbert and Privates Fox and Leavitt of the Second Cavalry.

We started in some style, Sergeant Gilbert and myself in the lead, Leavitt driving the team, and Private Fox as rear guard. Pack mules were dispensed with on this trip, much to our satisfaction, and the light wagon conveyed our luggage and provisions. We went up the

Tongue River to Pumpkin Creek, where an enforced halt was made to secure a loose tire, which gave us a lot of trouble until the wood had swelled sufficiently to hold it. With the aid of some wire which happened to be in the wagon temporary repairs were made by binding the tire to the felloe, and thereafter the wheel was taken off every night and given a good soaking to tighten it.

We crossed Pumpkin and Mizpah creeks and camped on Powder. After leaving the valley of the Powder, I laid a course in the direction of the Black Hills, or as nearly so as the nature of the country permitted, for one object of the expedition was to find a feasible route from the Yellowstone to the mining camp of Deadwood. Antelopes and buffaloes appeared in sight as we advanced across a rolling country which I do not remember well, though much of it appeared to embrace a choice stock range, with farming lands along the watered valleys. At one point of the journey, while ascending a gulch toward the divide where we surmised a first view of the Black Hills might offer, we stopped to examine some curious petrifactions of marine life which occurred in strata along one side of the gulch.

From the divide the Black Hills loomed in dark mass. At their foot we crossed the Belle Fourche, a shallow, gravelly stream of mountain water, and to the left entered a freshly made wagon road that wound along the right side of the valley through which flows Deadwood Creek, a road of easy grade with here and there marks of placer workings in the bottom land. This was the first road or wagon trail we touched after leaving Powder River, nor was there sign of habitation anywhere save old camp grounds or sites of Indian villages.

About midday we saw some scattered huts and tents

at the entrance of a rather narrow gulch, indicating the beginning of a mining camp, and the town of Deadwood was before us. At that day there were few buildings that could be called pretentious, but our attention was at once attracted by the sight of a powerful hydraulic hose and nozzle in operation that required the combined efforts of two men to handle. It threw a stream of water against the side of a high bank or hill, washing down tree stumps and roots and moving rocks that must have weighed a ton, as if they were blocks of wood.

An enterprising reporter for the leading paper in town interviewed me, and I have the result, clipped from the next day's paper, showing that the young man made the best of his opportunity. It reads as follows:

Mr. L. S. Kelly, better known on the border as "Yellowstone Kelly," the scout, accompanied by Sergeant Gilbert and Privates Fox and Leavitt of the Second Cavalry, arrived in the city yesterday. The expedition is traveling under the direction of General Miles, for the purpose of viewing the proposed military route from the mouth of the Tongue River to Deadwood, and making a report of its practicability as a route of travel from the Yellowstone and Powder River countries. Mr. Kelly finds the distance from the mouth of the Tongue River to Deadwood less than two hundred miles, and says for most part his route was through the *terra incognita* of the West, and laid open to view one of the finest grazing and farming districts yet explored. He says the road through is almost a natural one, save that portion that runs through the "bad lands" or *mauvis terres* of the Missouri. Much fine timber, many beautiful streams, and some wonderful natural rock formations were encountered. The country abounds in petrifactions, the most curious and attractive; the region is a paradise of game, and no

Indians or fresh Indian tracks were seen on the trail. Mr. Kelly's opinion, which is entitled to much weight, he having been in the employ of General Miles the past two years, and with that gallant officer during his Nez Percé campaign, is that this section of country has little to fear from Sitting Bull's forces the coming season, as none of his marauding bands will be able to leave their present rendezvous without receiving a heavy and terrible blow from General Miles' command. From a frontier acquaintance with "Yellowstone Kelly," the scout, which has traversed nearly a dozen years and has been mingled with many Indian experiences on the Missouri, the writer with pleasure attests his bravery, intelligence, and courtesy. After resting the stock a couple of days the expedition will return to Tongue River, taking in another supposed practicable route on the way.

Our light wagon, having a newly set tire, was ready for the trail. After crossing the Belle Fourche we turned to the left and entered that great plain that gives a view of the Devil's Tower, that black rock, or collection of rocks, that stands out from the mountain, of gloomy aspect when in shadow, but often fantastical under sunlight and heat waves from the plain. But we were miles and miles away from it and always bearing to the right. We saw buffalo bulls and tried to approach them, but the ground was too level. They were canny beasts and commanded all the shallow dry swales made by storm floods. Antelopes, of which there were many, proved easier and we had our usual feasts.

Powder River was high and unfordable. Casting about for a place to cross, since we had on hand a wagon to consider, a considerable detour was made, which took us some distance from any practicable direct route to the mouth of Tongue River. Finally, we came to a rope

Northward to the Border

ferry which gave access to a military camp under Captain Pollock, to whom I reported my presence and business. Captain Pollock informed me that Colonel Merritt with the Fifth Cavalry was coming to select the site for a new military post in the vicinity, and that his arrival was expected any moment. We therefore hastened to get away, for fear that our wagon and team might be commandeered for the use of the cavalry.

Sergeant Gilbert, who had been along the Bozeman trail before, showed me the site of old Fort Phil Kearny, under the shadow of a ridge, with nothing left but a fragment of the flagpole prone in the dust.[1] We passed along with bare prairie on the right and on our left wooded ravines carved out of the foothills of the Big Horn Mountains. Once more we camped near a rushing mountain torrent, and if hostile Indians had been about, such as roamed the land a twelve-month earlier, they might have walked into camp without our hearing them. Without incident of any kind we traveled down Tongue River to Fort Keogh, where I turned the team and light wagon over to the quartermaster in better shape than I had received them, and hastening to headquarters, made my report of the journey.

[1] Fort Phil Kearny, established in 1866 and abandoned in 1868, underwent a practically continuous state of siege during the two-year period of its occupancy, featured by some of the most determined fighting in the annals of Indian warfare. A spirited narrative of these events is Mrs. Frances Carrington's *My Army Life and the Fort Phil Kearny Massacre* . . . (Philadelphia, 1910).— ED.

CHAPTER XIII

SCOUTING IN YELLOWSTONE PARK

SOMEWHAT later in the season I made a trip to Yellowstone Park. I still have the original order I received for this mission, and since it explains the object of the journey I present it here:

HEADQUARTERS, DISTRICT OF THE YELLOWSTONE,
ACTING ASSISTANT ADJUTANT GENERAL'S OFFICE,

Fort Keogh, M.T. July 10th, 1878.

Scout L. S. Kelly,
    Fort Keogh, M.T.
Sir:

Yourself, Sergeant Gilbert, and one man will proceed without delay and follow up a party of prospectors and ascertain if they are trespassing on the Crow reservation; you will also ascertain what parties are infringing upon the rights of the Crow Indians and any information you may glean on these matters you will report to the district commander. You will also endeavor to ascertain if the Bannocks, or their allies, are making any movement eastwardly and should they do so you will report the fact to the nearest post and the District Commander without delay.

Should you need supplies you will go to Fort Custer or Ellis for them and the commanding officers of these posts are hereby respectfully requested to furnish you any assistance you may require.

Very respectfully, Your Obdt. Servant,

FRANK D. BALDWIN,
First Lieut., Fifth Infantry, A.D.C., A.A.A. Gen.

212

In Yellowstone Park

These directions covered considerable territory. Our quest for the prospectors might lead us a long way from the Bannock, and vice versa. When last heard from the Bannock were still west of the park and supposed to be in hiding in the mountains. I had spent many years in Montana and Dakota, but the region of country west of the Big Horn Mountains was still an unknown quantity, and at that day was used mostly by the mountain Crows and the Arapaho as a hunting ground. Before starting on this trip I went to the office of General Miles. I met him on the walk in front of his quarters and after some conversation he gave me the following additional order, which I still retain:

Fort Keogh, Montana,
July 10, 1878.

Any officer or steamboat captain having government forage can supply the government horses and Yellowstone Kelly's scouting party with grain, taking his receipt.

N. A. MILES,
Col. U.S.A., Comg. District.

The preparations for our trip were quickly made, our first objective point being Yellowstone Lake, whence I intended to go to Fort Ellis or Bozeman for supplies and then return to the west side of the lake and the geyser basin, in case we did not pick up the Bannock trail en route. The third member of our party was a friend of Sergeant Gilbert, a first sergeant in another troop, who wanted to go on this expedition.

Gilbert was a quiet, amiable man, a skilled hunter, whose delight it was to get away from the irksome discipline of a headquarters command. The other man (whose name I do not now recall) was a disciple of

213

Izaak Walton, and kept the camp supplied with trout whenever we were near a mountain stream. Besides our saddle horses we had three extra mounts to pack our blankets and supplies. Our course led up the Yellowstone Valley to the mouth of the Big Horn and thence up that stream to Fort Custer. Here we remained a day to draw supplies and rest our horses for the arduous task of penetrating the wilderness of mountains which form a barrier along the eastern limit of the park, with no road but the chance game trails, and where but few white men had preceded us.

We might have gone a shorter route across country to Fort Custer, but for the most part it is a rough and uninteresting region, hard on horses, and I wanted to see what changes had come over the valley in the two years of military occupation. In this I was disappointed, for there was little settlement below the mouth of the Big Horn on the north side; above that point embryo towns were in the course of building, with here and there farms in the making.

Fort Custer was built on a bare bluff which commanded a fine view of the mountains to the west. The Big Horn Mountains are usually enveloped in a soft blue haze when seen at a distance, and the effect is fine. On a nearer approach the peaks and pinnacles stand out in clear and rugged outline like stately sentinels of the landscape.

Our first day's ride led over the mesas and prairies along the foothills of the Big Horn Mountains, with beautiful stretches of grass and a profusion of wild flowers on every side; colors that harmonized with the brown rocks, as did the graceful antelopes that rose from the tall grass or started from some hidden ravine and scudded swift as the wind to a safe distance. Early in the afternoon we selected our camping ground for the night near a foaming little brook, under the shadow of the pine trees with a carpet of grass and pine needles.

About twenty-five miles from the Big Horn, at a point where it leaves the Black Canyon, we entered Pryor Pass, which gives upon the huge basin ringed by the Wind River Mountains and the mountains east of Yellowstone Lake. Looking west, the plain extends to the sheer wall of mountains that run north to the valley of the Yellowstone. The cuts in this wall show the canyons of the Stinking River, Clark's Fork, the Stillwater, and Rocky Fork. To the south may be seen Washakie's Needles, a group of slender peaks named after a Shoshone chief; to the east, the dark, gloomy entrance to the Black Canyon, and above it, Cloud Peak with its cap of perpetual snow.

Clark's Fork is noted as the scene of one phase of the retreat of the Nez Percés in the fall of 1877. Starting from Idaho, these Indians had made their way under great difficulties through Montana and the fastnesses of the mountains around Yellowstone Park. Pursued by the columns under General Howard, they forced their way with great courage through more than one column of troops sent to intercept them. When they reached Clark's Fork and were about to debouch upon the plain they found General Sturgis with the Seventh Cavalry in possession of the only outlet. With Howard pressing on in hot pursuit, the day looked dark enough for this intrepid band of aborigines. They extricated themselves from their desperate situation by a clever feint. Showing themselves to the cavalry, they slowly retired along a high ridge, disappearing behind it. Surmising that they were about to escape to the southward through some other gap in the mountains, General Sturgis marched his command in that direction along the base of the mountains, and when he was out of sight behind Heart Butte the Nez Percés, who were closely watching his movements, took advantage of the open way, and reaching the plain, pressed on to the Yellowstone. When Sturgis, after making a considerable detour, regained the trail, he found himself in the rear of Howard's command. Two days later the Seventh Cavalry came up with the retreating Indians as they entered a canyon on the north side of the Yellowstone and promptly attacked them, but were repulsed, as the Nez Percés had the advantage of position.

From Pryor Gap we passed to the Stinking River Canyon, whose gorge could be seen like a knife-cleft in the side of the mountain. The stream itself, bare of timber, is a beautiful mountain torrent of clear sparkling water where it issues out of the canyon. It receives its name from a small geyser which impregnates the water and the air with sulphureted hydrogen. The walls of the canyon are composed of a beautiful granite, and I noticed a cap of limestone. A couple of gentlemanly prospectors whom we met here, who had pitched their tent for the day near the water's edge, expressed the opinion that it was useless to look for gold near a limestone ledge, or where there was a limestone cap. I could not then gainsay the statement, but I have since, in Nevada, mined in rock charged with copper elements and also carrying gold, that was frozen to a ledge of limestone.

Learning that there was a small camp of prospectors somewhere along the face of the mountain, I rode up there accompanied by one of the other men. It proved to be the tail end of what was known as the "Whitmore stampede." The story goes that years before, when it was not safe to travel in these mountains, a miner of that name had found a rich prospect; he had been compelled to leave, and when he returned with a strong party he could not find the place he had located. Now, here he was again with a following from the Black Hills, miners, lawyers, even judges, eager for the quest. Whitmore, with two men, had gone in search of the find, the rest of the party remaining in camp awaiting their return.

As the discovery prospect was manifestly off the Crow Reservation I did not see any reason for disturbing these people. Their camp was in a little ravine near Heart Butte, and I found them in a very bad plight, for the camp had been visited by a cloudburst a night or two before that had washed away most of their provisions and baggage. I saw rocks that weighed half a ton, which had been moved by the sudden rush of water.

Before returning to camp we made a detour through the mountains, much of it almost impassable for horses. On the summit we stopped for awhile to watch the odd maneuvers of a black bear on a snowbank. He appeared to be raking in something with his claws, which he devoured with much gusto. Finally, our curiosity was so excited that we moved toward him to see what he was eating. As there were fresh elk sign in the vicinity we had no intention of firing at the bear. Of course he stampeded as soon as we came into view, ambling off in the usual ludicrous manner, turning his head first on one side and then on the other to watch us. We found that the snowbank was literally covered with grasshoppers, which had become benumbed in crossing the range. At the edge of the snowbank, where it was melting, the water carried down quantities of the hoppers to where the trout lurked around the mouths of small streams.

From our point of observation the vista stretched up the north fork of the Stinking River and was altogether lovely, wild, and picturesque. The sharp, pine-clad ridges sloped gently to the valley, the dark green foliage of which was dotted with groves of the brighter-tinted aspen and cottonwood.

I quickly decided that this valley was the course to the lake, and surmised that it could not be more than twenty miles beyond where our view terminated. As we descended the mountain to the north fork we saw two horsemen riding rapidly in our direction. While awaiting their approach we saw that a camp had been formed on the river bank near the forks, about a mile distant, where the valley opened out to form a little park above the narrow canyon.

The riders proved to be an officer from Fort Washakie and the guide, McCabe, from that post. The officer, with a party of cavalry, was looking for two deserters. Seeing my companion, who was in uniform, they naturally thought they had come up with their quarry, until upon a nearer approach they saw their mistake. As our course lay at right angles to the one they were pursuing we had dismounted to await their coming. The officer asked me where I was from. I replied, "Fort Keogh," adding that we were out under orders from the district commander. He then told me the object of their search.

They soon moved on and we struck a bee line over the mountains to our camp, which, like most short cuts in a wild country, involved double the labor and fatigue

"YELLOWSTONE KELLY"

"THE-LITTLE-MAN-WITH-A-STRONG-HEART"

we would have encountered by traversing the smoother and more roundabout trail, besides compelling us to camp out another night. We regretted, then, that we had not gone to the cavalry camp and enjoyed their hospitality for the night instead of wearing ourselves out in toiling over the rocks and through the chaparral of the mountains. We reached our camp early the next morning and soon prepared to push on to the lake.

Winding along the north fork of this mountain stream was a pleasant diversion, for here the game trails led, ever upward, through the cool sequestered woods of pine and aspen which bordered the tiny streams. Early in the afternoon we camped in a little park of grass and flowers and feasted on coffee, trout, and venison, flanked by cans of condensed milk and currant jelly.

After this repast I picked up my rifle and was soon lost in the forest primeval of the narrowing valley. In this tangled wilderness I was keen to find the trail to Yellowstone Lake. On either side were strata of red rock overtopped with lava formation, the red and gray of which contrasted with the mountain's vegetation. The way became steeper and soon with one long spurt I gained the summit and throwing myself breathless on the ground gazed long at the beautiful view spread out before me. Below was the lake at a distance of ten or twelve miles, like a gem of silver in an emerald setting; beyond, the continental divide, with the Three Tetons looming dark and misty to the left in the distance, jagged and capped with snow. With my glasses I could see whitecaps on the lake, snow-white flocks of pelicans, and steam rising from some geysers on the east shore of the lake. Reluctantly I turned away from this enchanting view and retraced my steps to camp, on the way shooting a noble buck, whose horns were in velvet.

The ascent to the summit of the pass the next morning was very toilsome and in some places we were obliged to cut our way through the tangled chaparral. While doing this a band of elk started in plain view and we ceased our labor a moment to watch them. The male is a very stately animal, as with head thrown back and nose in the air he trots through the timber like a true monarch of the forest. On the summit, while our horses were getting their second wind, we stayed to examine the country ahead, then descended through the pines to the lake shore and camped near a pond where the timber was open, with no underbrush.

One of the men reported that he had seen a beaver asleep on a stump in a small lake near by; this I thought so odd that I took my gun and walked down to the place. The animal was still on the stump when I got there, but it did not look like a beaver. I fired and he disappeared like a flash in the water. I was able to reach the stump and after waiting a moment saw a shadow in the water, and reaching down I brought to the surface a fine otter. Quite elated, I carried it back to camp and soon had the pelt stretched on a willow frame.

From our camp we made our way down to the foot of the lake, forded the outlet at a shallow place, and made for the head of the main finger on the west side of the lake, keeping close watch, meanwhile, for Indian signs, although I did not expect to find any so far away from the main trails leading to the Clark's Fork country. Skirting the lake, we wandered to the left a mile or two and found a tiny lake from which we drew a salmon, an indication that its waters emptied into some tributary of the Snake. The country was quite flat and heavily wooded with pine.

We kept on to the foot of Mount Sheridan, where we camped near two tiny springs, one hot and one cold. Leaving my companions to look after the camp, with orders to do no shooting, I ascended the mountain, which I found bare and rocky, and from the summit had a fine view of the surrounding country. Long and earnestly I swept the country with my glasses for signs of smoke or Indian tents, but there was no sign of life except the white swans and pelicans on the lake, which from this point showed plainly the fingers and thumb characteristics of this body of water. Descending to our camp, I removed the ban on shooting; Gilbert promptly killed a fine buck and we had meat galore for two or three days.

I had a desire to essay the direct passage through the wilderness to the geyser basin, but I had been informed that it was very difficult. Indeed, I learned that Captain Jones of the engineers with a party from Fort Washakie had made the attempt and had succeeded in getting through only after many mishaps in a maze of windfalls of fallen timber. However, we had our work cut out for us in finding that elusive camp of Bannock, if the drive of these Indians eastward should prove a reality and not merely a surmise.

Midday found us near the outlet of the lake, that silent stream flowing smoothly to where it gained headway near the upper falls, and past the paint-pot holes with their ceaseless plop, plop, more distracting than the noise of a roaring cataract. Pursuing our way along the river trail, we suddenly came to the lower falls of the Yellowstone, where the river drops with a cloud of spray into a gleaming yellow-walled canyon, down which it frisks until lost to view.

There was no sign of Indians or of a fresh trail at the only crossing at Baronett's bridge, nor along the east fork of the Yellowstone leading to Clark's Fork and the open country; nor could we glean any information at the Mammoth Hot Springs, where Norris, the superintendent of the park, had his headquarters. In the chill mist of early morning we passed like ghosts along a rude road into the geyser basin. The steam rising from the pent waters seemed a part of the mist. We could see but a short distance ahead and did not know what we were missing, but we heard the roar of a geyser in close proximity. The trail had disappeared and we were treading a crust formed by steaming subterranean waters, a crust that sounded hollow and was hot to the touch. I dismounted and led my horse carefully around the thin places for fear he would break through and scald his legs.

We traveled in this way for a mile or more, stopping at one point to admire a deep pool whose cerulean depths were lost in darkness. Another mound-like pool that boiled and threatened to explode in our faces, but never did, was a natural laundry, for we later found that a foul and sweated saddle blanket, thrown into its engulfing maw, was churned into cleanliness in short order. As we moved along, charmed by the sights on either hand, the morning sun shining over the tops of the pines pierced the mist and disclosed to our gaze Old Faithful, a tall rugged mound gleaming in grays and whites from a recent display of its spouting column.

There came a throbbing in the inner throat of the geyser, producing an increasing violence in its steamy depth that forced a mass of boiling water above the rim and before this could sink back it was forced to a greater height where it hung for a moment undecided to sustain its cohesion, when with a roar like wild beasts breaking all restraint in a mad dash for freedom, a solid column of the churned water rose high into the air, breaking away but always reinforced by succeeding columns until, exhausted by the accelerating and stupendous effort, it returned slowly upon itself while all about a flood ebbed four ways, leaving little douches of mineral to build and maintain those beautiful cup-like troughs or channels of delicate hues which are peculiar to this formation.

We returned through the park by another route and found that the Bannock had slipped through despite our watchfulness (we had a hundred miles or more to cover) and had been intercepted and captured by General Miles, who was on his way to the park with a party of friends and guests and a detachment of soldiers as escort. Learning that the Bannock had crossed the mountains, he hastily changed his plans and sending his party to Fort Ellis, intercepted the Bannock with the aid of some mountain Crows, and in an early morning skirmish killed a number of them and captured the rest. Captain Bennett of the Fifth Infantry was killed in this action. The Crows, as usual, got away with the ponies.

General Miles and his party later camped near the lower falls of the Yellowstone, where we reported to him. Idling here even amidst such beautiful surroundings became monotonous, and together with the two cavalry sergeants, nothing loath, I hit the trail for new scenes of exploration. I am not sure if it was in the fall of this year or in the following one that at the instance of the superintendent of Yellowstone Park, Mr. Norris, I went to meet a troop of cavalry en route from Camp Brown, Wyoming, to the park to act as escort to the Reeves Boundary Survey, charged with the duty of surveying the west line of the park.

I was alone in camp on the west side of the Stinking River Pass when in the clear air of early morning I heard voices and the shuffling footsteps of horses approaching. I recognized the voice of the one talking, and going a little way from my camp toward them, I concealed myself behind a tree and when they had passed a few yards beyond me I stepped out and in a ringing voice ordered them to halt. They proved to be George Towne, a trapper whom I had seen a few days before at Mammoth Hot Springs, and Mr. Seymour, an artist from New York City, who was making sketches in the country. The message that Towne brought from the superintendent was not very clear as to the whereabouts of the troops of cavalry, but I surmised that they would naturally come down the river above the lake.

At this time there were practically no trails in the park aside from game trails, only a rough track connecting the geyser basin with Mammoth Hot Springs. The east side of the lake was heavily timbered, with considerable underbrush. It was not easy traveling and the course I took, as nearly straight to the head of the lake as was feasible, was rough enough. To add to my troubles, Mr. Seymour would persist in stopping to sketch whenever he saw a likable contour or a promontory head, and I was more than once obliged to halt or go back after him, for once lost he might be lost for good.

When I had gained the head of the lake and had traversed a mile or two of the upper Yellowstone River, which here was not much of a stream, I decided to cross and see if there was a fresh trail on the other side. Here we found a fresh horse and mule trail going down stream. After we had followed it a couple of miles it turned off into a swamp nearer the river. Here it meandered around, as though the people who made it were lost, then it led back to high ground, and very soon we came to a cavalry camp in a little opening. Inquiring for the officer in command, I was told that Captain ———— had gone ahead to look up the trail.

I went into camp, tired enough with the day's journey. In about an hour I met the captain, a fine-looking, stocky cavalryman, who said that he had been trying to pick up the tracks of the surveyors, who had gone ahead to the geyser basin, leaving their burro pack train with his command. He added that he expected to join the surveyors at the basin and was glad that now someone was along to show them the way.

It did not look easy to me, for I knew that there was no trail from the west side of the lake. Indeed, report made it a jumble of down timber, and the most experienced guides in bringing tourists from the entrance to the park, Mammoth Hot Springs, to the lake returned by the same route to Mary's Lake, or some other point, to where a trail diverged to the geyser basin.

An early start was made the next morning. The troop had a fine pack train of mules and I wondered how the surveyors' train of burros could keep up and surmount such obstacles as fallen trees and logs. We had traveled barely eight miles and had reached a pleasant halting place when I proposed to the captain to camp, while I went ahead to look out a course through the wilderness.

He seemed surprised, smiled, and said, "Why, we have only come a short distance, seven or eight miles."

"Yes," I replied, "but there is some bad traveling ahead for the packs that I wish to avoid." He consented without further question, and I went ahead and had progressed about half a mile when I ran plump onto a big bull elk lying down in the shade of a tree.

The elk had scarcely gained his feet when he fell with a bullet in his heart. I waited long enough to open him and remove most of the viscera, then I returned to camp and the captain sent out two pack mules and packers for the meat. They were mighty glad to get that meat, and the packers told me that the troop had killed nothing in the way of fresh meat since leaving Camp Brown, but had lived mostly on fish. I then went on and finished my survey and returned to camp, satisfied that we could make the west side of the lake without much difficulty.

In the evening the company cooks set to work making bread with the last of the supply of flour. A trench one foot in depth having been dug by the soldiers and partly filled with red-hot coals, the cooks at the proper time, having filled a large number of iron mess-pans with raised or baking-powder dough, placed the pans in the trench and covered each with another and slightly larger pan. Hot ashes and coals were then heaped upon the pans, the whole being then covered with turf.

I was not present when the trench was uncovered in the morning and the loaves removed, but I saw them later, when the morning meal was served, light and beautiful bread, crisp to the touch when broken, sweet and wholesome as any that ever came out of an oven, with a nutty flavor born of the compressed steam that enveloped them in their earth prison. This soldier-made bread was an unusual treat with elk meat, steam-roasted in a Dutch oven furnished for the occasion by the civilian cook of the surveyors' pack train.

Driving straight through the primeval woods where the going was good, weaving in and out of patches of fallen timber and making detours where forced to, the long line of horsemen and packs made a heavy trail, for all traveled in single file, the mules stopping to nibble at the wayside brush and then racing each other to get second place to the bell mare that led the train and scared all game within sound of its brazen appendage. The burro train coming behind found a ready-made trail, their packs striking the trees on either side a few inches lower than the mules.

We made one of the fingers of the lake and camped at the head, where a water avenue afforded a charming view of the lake. I was now approaching ground that was familiar. We were not so far from the foot of Mount Sheridan that I could fail to sense landmarks. I knew that between the base of the mountain and the lake there was a swamp, of what extent I could only surmise, but I thought proper to make a detour and avoid it. This we did and I was soon on the course pursued earlier in the summer when with the two cavalry sergeants I passed along the west side of the lake looking for the Bannock. We were now out of the wilderness, though still in the woods. The somber forest lay all about. Early in the day we came to the spot on the west side of the lake, of dubious repute, where a man might throw for a trout and without changing his position swing the trout, still on the hook, to a spot where it is cooked in the boiling water of a hot spring issuing from the shallow bottom.

"Yellowstone Kelly"

From this point we were to leave the lake and penetrate an untraveled and unknown forest to reach the geyser basin. I was confident that we could make it, but expected to strike very rough going. That piece of country had an evil reputation. Alone, or with a companion, I should have liked nothing better than to attempt it. We went into camp by the lakeside—a poor place, there being little or no feed.

Bright and early next morning we were on the way, I in the lead, the captain following at the head of his troop in column of twos. When next I looked back the troop had changed to a single line, the end of which could not be seen. We passed a pretty lake with a meadow around it, crossed some little ridges, and soon came in sight of a little cloud, straight ahead of us, which on closer approach proved to be Old Faithful, spouting for our entertainment. We rode around a little knoll to the left, crossed a gulch and the Firehole River, and found ourselves in the upper geyser basin.

Mr. Norris, the superintendent, immediately dispatched a construction party to cut out and build a temporary roadway along the course of our trail. I say he hastened to do this, fearing, mayhap, that otherwise the trail might disappear and leave no trace to guide the eager tourists whom he expected in shoals to view the sights of this wondrous region. Kind, amiable gentleman, a man of parts, he took an interest in me and would have me walk with him of an evening at our camps in the park, ostensibly to view the beauties of nature but mostly, I suspected, to wear off some of his nervous temper. He had a penchant for odd things, as witness his road of glass on the way to the Firehole Basin, where a ledge of black obsidian obtruded, which he wore into shape by building fires and when the glassy mineral was well heated pouring water on it.

The winter of 1879-1880 was bitterly cold. In December the buffaloes left their winter ranges along the base of the Bear Paw Mountains and Milk River and, drifting south, vast herds were massed in the valley of the Yellowstone in January, on the plain opposite the mouth of Powder River. The cold wave extended far into the north. The allied Sioux gathered around Sitting Bull's camp near the Burnt Wood Mountain north of Milk River suffered from this movement of the larger game, for their chief dependence for food in those days was on buffalo meat. Many of their ponies had perished and the intense cold had daunted the ardor even of the young men who formed the predatory winter war parties of the region.

In February there came a mild chinook that warmed the air and made water of the snow, and the hordes of buffaloes overcame their fear of the white man's road, crossed to the south bank, and were gone, and I suspect but few came back from that south country, swarming with Indians and hide hunters.

But before their departure I had an opportunity to see this great plain when it was covered by masses of these wild and picturesque beasts, to the number of half a million or more. In February a hunting party of soldiers from Fort Keogh with two or three wagons were on their way to this ground when I joined them. The weather was so cold and calm that the smoke from a camp fire rose in a slender black thread high into the air.

We approached a little bottom with the intention of camping, and found that a bunch of young bulls occupied the ground. It was so cold that they refused to move and the soldiers killed enough to fill the wagons. We made camp by putting two A tents close together so that the openings faced, and entrance was effected by pulling the two ends of the tents apart and squeezing through. Of course the little Sibley stove stood here, the pipe thrust through a tin protector at the top, the entire combination forming one long tent with a stove in the center. When a fire was burning in the stove the tent was uncomfortably warm, but as the fire died down the bitter air rushed in from all sides. To cook a meal in the cramped funnel-shaped space around the stove required great ingenuity.

The butchering of the buffaloes we had killed required the use of bare hands and proved a troublesome job. Handling the warm flesh and hot viscera was easy, but the outside work called for the use of mittens. We removed the paunch and entrails and left each carcass in shape to drain. This was a great mistake, as it should have been quartered for easy handling in loading. The consequence was that in the morning when we came to load the wagons we found the meat frozen so hard that an axe in the hands of a soldier made little impression on it, and meat and hide slivered off like ice. The thermometer that morning at the post hospital forty miles away registered fifty degrees below zero.

My old friend, Sandy Morris, whom I had accompanied to the base of the Bear Paw Mountains after his partner, George Horn, had been killed, was trapping on Powder River with a new partner when they discovered fresh moccasin tracks one morning in the valley and hastily retreated down the river, where they made camp in the bottom where drift slabs and poles had collected, of which they built themselves a substantial breastwork.

Early on the following morning, while they were eating breakfast, six Indians suddenly appeared in the adjacent timber with evident hostile intent. Sandy motioned them to keep off, whereupon one of the party laid down his rifle and advanced with his hands extended. He was allowed to enter the little corral and while Sandy was talking to him his companion kept an eye on the other Indians, who were partially concealed by the timber. Now Sandy, as I have reason to know, while true blue in contact with hostile Indians, was nervous and trembled like a man with the ague. It may be that the Indian noticed this agitation on Sandy's part and was rendered desperate by the situation, for when some suspicious movement among the other Indians attracted Sandy's attention for a moment he suddenly seized the rifles the two men held in their hands. Had the other Indians rushed in then it would have been the end of the two white men.

In the scuffle that ensued both men fell to the ground with the Indian on top. Sandy's Winchester went off accidentally, grazing him on the wrist, but he finally managed to extricate himself and gun and shot the Indian in the stomach. The Indian jumped over the corral and disappeared among the trees before Sandy could get another cartridge into the chamber of his Winchester. A skirmishing fire ensued during which Sandy shot another Indian, who exposed a dusky head from behind a tree. Shortly after this the Indians retired and the two white men made haste to reach the fort, a distance of about forty miles.

On hearing their story General Miles ordered out a

small detachment of soldiers under command of a corporal of cavalry who had had some success in following Indians. The party comprised seven cavalrymen or mounted infantry, about the same number of our Cheyenne allies, Sandy, myself, and one other civilian. A late start was made and it was dark before we had traversed more than two-thirds of the distance to Powder River. I still remember that dark moonless night and the rough trail we followed.

Arriving about midnight at the scene of the encounter, the horses and mules were attended to and disposition was at once made for repose. We were astir very early in the morning, breakfast was prepared, the saddle horses and pack mules were fed, blankets folded, and all impedimenta packed for an early departure to follow the trail of the Indians, not a difficult matter in the soft ground of that thawing period.

Meanwhile, my attention was drawn to a young Cheyenne scout prowling around in the timber, who uttered a low exclamation, and drawing near, we discovered under a pile of brush a dead Indian wrapped in his blanket with a bullet-hole between his eyes. Further exploration revealed the fact that the Indian who had been wounded in the corral had turned back to his home country accompanied by one of his companions, as shown by the tracks, leaving three of the six to continue their quest and divert possible pursuers from their wounded comrade.

The tracks of the three Sioux led up Powder River. By sunrise we were on the trail, which was easy to follow, as the February sun thawed the snow sufficiently to retain the clear impress of any track, which the frosty nights froze into rigidity. They were already trapped, for they could not conceal their footsteps.

We had not traveled more than ten miles when it became apparent that the Sioux realized that they would be followed, for they would take advantage of every slope or ridge that was bare of snow, and twice they left their direct course to travel along the bed of gulches down which trickled little streams of snow water, expecting that the flow of water would increase in volume and wash out the tracks. In one place they had doubled on their tracks and had camped in a little hollow which formed an excellent ambush from which to strike any who might pass. The Cheyenne pointed to this spot significantly and laughed as they rode by.

From this point on we were more deliberate in our manner of travel and took turns in riding ahead. We had left the Powder River Valley and were traversing the broken ridges that border the Mizpah; the way became more difficult and broken cliffs appeared on either side, covered with the stunted cedar and pine of that locality and frequented by mountain sheep and blacktail deer. Late in the day we made camp in a grassy hollow, the Cheyenne a little apart, as our party was too large to find comfort around one camp fire.

All appeared to be in good spirits that evening for there was some excitement in the chase, though the advantage was clearly in our favor. After supper the Indians sat in a circle around their little fire, and passing the pipe from one to another, sang in low tones snatches of song, which must have been of a humorous nature as it was frequently interrupted by laughter.

The corporal interrogated one of the Cheyenne, whom I will call Yellow Bull, as to the probability of our overtaking the Sioux. He expressed the opinion that we would come up with them about noon of the next day. This he expressed in the graceful gestures of the sign language, then added in the Yankton Sioux dialect (which is generally used in the region of the upper Missouri by the different tribes in their intercourse with the whites), *Kichesapa eba duxya*—"They will fight." This was a foregone conclusion with nearly all. Only a short time before these same Cheyenne scouts had been hostile Indians and had doubtless been in much the same predicament as the Sioux ahead. With the instinct of a savage every detail of the chase was clear to Yellow Bull; every artifice used approved itself to his understanding, and he probably knew the very spot or points from which the Sioux would watch the pursuit.

By daylight we were on the trail. The way became rougher as we advanced and the raw February wind swept down from the gulches with chilling force. Troops of black-tail deer sped away from our front into the cedar groves, but no one fired a shot. About noon, as we were traversing a grassy glade, the wind, which swept through every hollow and apparently from no particular direction, wafted to us the odor of burning sage. At once all were on the alert. The Cheyenne scattered out to find the quarry; we followed suit and some little time had elapsed, for we moved with extreme caution, knowing the artifices these fellows resorted to, when my attention was attracted by the movements of one of the Cheyenne scouts who stood behind Douglass, one of the cavalrymen, pointing eagerly ahead in a manner to encourage the soldier to advance while he followed in the rear. Just at that moment a shot was fired from the gulch ahead killing Douglass almost instantly. He lunged forward over the bank and fell in the sage brush. The Cheyenne dropped instantly and remained motionless for a time before he dared to move; then with strange contortions of the body he exerted himself slowly and slipped away without exposing himself to a shot.

There was more or less confusion for a bit, during which shots were exchanged between some of our party, who had crossed a ravine onto an opposite rise of ground, and the Sioux, who were concealed in a sort of ice cave under a large rock. A short distance from the rock their camp fire was visible, near which a couple of blankets had been flung down, showing that the Indians had been taken by surprise, though the camp had been made near the rock with a view to its possible use as a place of refuge. It was a sorry retreat for it was merely a hole large enough barely to conceal them, and desperate indeed was their situation without their blankets.

Fronting the ravine and facing this retreat, a hundred yards or more away, was the crest of a small hill that overlooked the ground in front. Thither the Cheyenne had betaken themselves, and in a short time a number of our party had congregated at the same point for consultation. One of the cavalrymen who ventured too close to the retreat of the Sioux received a shot in the breast, and as he was very weak it was thought best to send in to the post for a surgeon. A volunteer was called for to carry a dispatch; none of the Cheyenne responding, a young Sioux scout who was with the party stepped forward and offered to go. Apparently the matter was settled and the young man had gone to fetch his pony when the Cheyenne protested, representing that he was a

Sioux and not to be depended on for such a mission, and several now offered to go in his place.

The corporal stood irresolute with the scribbled note in his hand, and was about to give it to a Cheyenne. I, also, was momentarily stayed in my mind by the specious argument, but the young Sioux, sensing the situation, protested in his turn that he was an honorable warrior and would faithfully deliver the paper. The corporal being still undetermined, I came to his assistance, advising that the young man be employed for the service. The Indian put the dispatch in his pouch and jumping onto his pony made off at full speed over the hills.

The rest of the party now brought rocks and I crawled to the crest of the hill and built a protecting barrier from which to survey at ease the dark entrance of the retreat in which the Indians were concealed. When the barrier had attained sufficient height I made a porthole in it with enough cover to protect an observer. With my field glass I looked long and patiently, but could see nothing to shoot at but a shadowy hole. I soon gave place to Sandy, who at my suggestion elevated his old black sombrero on a gun stick just above the top of the lookout. They seemed to recognize his headgear and promptly plugged it with a bullet.

Tiring of this unprofitable hazard, we soon abandoned the place to our allies, who made persistent use of it. It was certain that the three Sioux were in wretched plight; huddled on the icy ground in a dark hole, without protection, having foolishly abandoned their blankets, sheer desperation would force them, as I believed, to make a break for liberty in the dark and get away.

In Yellowstone Park

Guards were placed in a circle to prevent their escape, and disposition for camp was made in a little hollow near the rise where Douglass had received his death wound. His body lay just over the rise, in full view and close to the retreat of the concealed warriors. I had thought of a plan to crawl to his body after darkness set in and secure his rifle, and if possible his belt of ammunition.

It was a cheerless camp; a raw, cutting wind prevailed and the night was dark, the moon showing but dimly through the drifting clouds. After we had eaten a scanty meal of bacon, hard-tack, and coffee I uncovered my plan and made ready with a light rope, one end of which I proposed to lug and attach to the body if it seemed feasible to drag it clear from any entangling obstruction. It was but a few steps from the fitful light of the camp fire and all followed to see the start. I borrowed a revolver, not being able to use my rifle to advantage in worming my way over the crest, where I might be observed from the front; but I did not fear this, for I saw that the cedars in our rear formed a background that would render me invisible to observation in the absence of light. Gaining the top, I lay motionless a moment trying to visualize the ground ahead, but it was all a blur. The rope proving too short for the purpose designed, I dropped the end which I held in my hand, and cautiously working along between the short shrubs and tufts of grass, came to where I could lay my hand on the foot of the dead soldier.

Raising myself slightly, I could discern the outline of the retreat. All was silent as the grave, save the wind sighing through the cedars. I could have thrown a stone against the rock that concealed them, as we did earlier in the day from the bank above them on the other side, but I had no desire to draw their attention. I could also see the rifle of the dead man, lying where it had pitched forward from the nerveless hand that could no longer retain it. In order to reach it I would be obliged to step over the body, take two steps, and make a quick grab and a quicker retreat. This I had no desire to do; it involved great risk for too little profit. On the other side of the cave were soldiers and Cheyenne on guard, watching for any attempt of the enemy to escape, and as they were not aware of my adventure any movement on my part might bring on me a volley from both friend and foe. I returned with utmost caution to the bivouac, much to the satisfaction of my friends, who did not approve of the risks that I ran.

Dawn found the camp astir, and while devouring our hastily cooked breakfast a scheme was devised to rout the Sioux from their nest under the rock. This scheme was simply to rush in a body on their retreat and kill them if they made resistance, otherwise to drag them out. This plan met the approval of our allies, the Cheyenne, though it is safe to say they had no intention of forming the van of such a venture. While getting ready for this attack, someone drew our attention to a body of Indians sweeping down in a swift gallop from the near-by hills. While considering them we soon perceived that they were followed by a column of mounted soldiers and we knew that our Sioux courier had lost no time in reaching Fort Keogh with his dispatch.

Captain Snyder of the Fifth Regiment with his company rode up, and learning how matters stood, sent White Bull, a Cheyenne chief, to parley with the Sioux and endeavor to persuade them to surrender. White

CHIEF WHITE BULL
Courtesy General Nelson A. Miles.

KICKING BEAR
Courtesy General Nelson A. Miles.

In Yellowstone Park

Bull took his stand on a small eminence and harangued the hollow some little time without eliciting any reply. Finally, a faint response came, then a short parley, and the way being made clear, our three hostiles came forth. The foremost one was a tall, sullen-looking fellow wrapped in a white Hudson's Bay blanket-coat with hood of the same material; the others were of the same type, but shorter and with stolid, impassive faces. They were all of a tremble, but not with fear, and it was painful to see the leader as he stood with arms folded tight against his breast while being interrogated.

The prisoners stated that they had come from Sitting Bull's camp near Woody Mountain, north of Milk River, and were on a horse-stealing expedition to their enemies, the mountain Crows, until the unfortunate affair when their leader was killed. After that they had continued their original course in a desperate attempt to deflect pursuit from their wounded comrade. One of the trio had received a shot in the leg while lying in the hole.

The wounded soldier was cared for by the surgeon and placed upon a horse. The dead one was wrapped in a canvas, lashed onto a pack mule, and so transported to the Yellowstone. Down the company street the cavalcade took its way, and then, in the presence of the post commander, company officers, and the company to which the man belonged, the body of the dead soldier was unlashed from the pack mule and delivered to his waiting comrades.

CHAPTER XIV

SCOUTING IN COLORADO

SPRING came on apace, and now, sure that peace reigned in the valley and the surrounding region, the old restlessness came over me and I felt impelled toward other fields of endeavor. It was not easy to part from old friends and acquaintances—the gallant officers and men with whom I had camped in fair weather and in foul, who had trusted me to guide them in unfamiliar and hostile country where often water, fuel, and grass were not combined or available for a considerable body of troops and their transport.

The great blank spaces on the map of this extensive region had now been filled with trails and wagon routes; hunters, stockmen, and prospective settlers roamed at will looking for locations. Even the red men who had fought us at Wolf Mountain and had surrendered in good faith to the military were contented in their camps under the observation of competent officers; while the hostile and turbulent element, under the leadership of Sitting Bull and other chiefs, were safe—as we then judged—across the border to the north, under the observation of the Dominion officers.

A steamer was leaving for the lower country and with my rifle and duffle bag in hand I walked aboard. Of that voyage down the Yellowstone and the Missouri I remember little, save that at Fort Berthold there was the usual throng of Indians on the high bank to view the passing show, always new, a custom that has prevailed probably since the day when the first peace treaty was made between the Arikara, Mandan, and Hidatsa more than one hundred years ago.

At last one day the stage from Georgetown, Colorado, crawling ever upward through the cooling pines, arrived finally in the cool atmosphere of Leadville, where a comfortable and roomy tent lodging received me and my slender belongings, the heaviest of which was my rifle. It was a relief and a pleasure to enter at once into a company of quiet, courteous men, all miners apparently, but men who had studied for the business before launching out into the rough and ready ways of typical mining camps. There were mining engineers, bearded fellows, who had seen service in military camps, experienced miners and prospectors, and graduates of schools of mines, in quiet discourse or reading books and papers.

I did not stay long in this mining camp. Having purchased a pony and some provisions, I climbed the ridge past the tiny twin lakes and traveled on across Boulder Creek to Aspen, another tent city in the making, prospecting and killing deer as I needed meat, for all of that region swarmed with deer, elk, and bear. On Plateau Creek, under the Grand Mesa, I ran into old Colorow, a Ute sub-chief, who was hunting deer all by himself. Like many another Indian, Colorow took a fancy to my rifle and offered two horses for it. My decisive refusal blocked any further parley on the subject.

This chief, with others, had been concerned in the killing of Mr. Meeker, the agent for the Utes, on White River in the preceding autumn. The Utes had been very insolent toward the agent and the whites generally for some time, and the Interior Department had asked that a military force make a demonstration in that direction with a view to placing the Indians on their good behavior.

In response to this call a column of cavalry under command of Major Thornburg marched rapidly from Rawlings, Wyoming, on the road to Bear River and was well into the Utes' country before the incensed Indians learned that an invasion was impending. A large war party under the leadership of Jack proceeded from the agency up the valley one day in the autumn of 1878 to where the road debouched from a narrow gulch, and turning up this thoroughfare they stopped behind a low ridge at one side of the road where a pony trail cuts the winding course of the gulch. Here they waited.

The column of cavalry was approaching, the commander in an ambulance at the head, the baggage wagons following. The air was crisp with the spell of the exhilarating altitude, for the spot lies on the western slope of the Rocky Mountains, where the waters flow to the Pacific Ocean. The road wound around a hollow, but the guide, either intentionally or by mistake, took the grass-grown Indian trail that led directly over the hill, a low divide that separates Bear River from White River. Bill Williams' Fork of Bear River lies over the hill, and here the ancient trapper used to trap and hunt the beaver which harnessed the streams in every direction in those days. Unconscious of the lurking Indians behind the ridge, the column came on. The Indians clutched their rifles in anticipation of the conflict, but kept their ponies well in hand ready to skip out if the venture failed.

A rifle shot rings out, then another. The Utes rise from their concealment and pour a volley into the troops as they ride up the slope. The soldiers, though taken by surprise, return the fire in some disorder. Major Thornburg is killed in his ambulance and the retirement that is ordered becomes a pursuit on the part of the Utes, who follow closely and fire from rock and brush, for they outnumber the soldiers two to one.

Meanwhile, the wagons, having unfortunately struck the most unfavorable spot in the entire gulch for defense, halted in their tracks and could not afterward be moved, for the Indians, grown bold by the success of their attack, surrounded the command and from behind the rocks and ridges that commanded the position of the soldiers poured in a steady fire, killing men, mules, and horses in rapid succession.

The troops defended themselves as best they could behind the protection afforded by the corralled wagons and entrenchments hastily constructed, until night closed the conflict. During the night Jack dispatched a swift messenger to the agency, where Colorow and Douglas, the chiefs proper, held sway, to inform them of the situation. The chiefs thereupon proceeded to kill Mr. Meeker and the other employees of the agency, and taking the women as prisoners withdrew to some fastness in the mountains.

Meanwhile, the troops were in a serious dilemma. They could not move to better ground, for the only water to be had was at their present camp, and they had many wounded men and no transportation left. So they made themselves as secure as possible and under cover of the darkness dispatched the guide to Rawlings for assistance.

The Utes conducted the siege in leisurely fashion, retiring at night to their bivouac and renewing the attack in the morning. A troop of negro cavalry on escort duty somewhere in the vicinity, learning of the desperate situation of Major Thornburg's command, rushed to the rescue and arrived early in the morning before the Utes had reappeared from their camp to harass the hemmed-in troops.

The fight went on in desultory fashion during the day, the Utes popping away at any object that showed among the wagons and the soldiers returning the compliment whenever the Indians skirted the crests of the hills on their fleet ponies, as they frequently did in bravado. After a siege of three or four days' duration, during which the wounded were in desperate shape, a relief column under command of General Merritt appeared on the scene and the Utes quickly vanished. They were never punished for this outbreak, unless the deprivation of their lands and curtailment of hunting privileges might be deemed a punishment.

Skirting the ridges that look down on Grand River, I came to the heads of Plateau Creek, a beautiful region, but not a place to look for gold. What did I care? Being heart and mind free, I gave myself up to the joy of living and camped in the shadow of aspens in lovely spots where deer and elk were abundant. I had killed a buck and I hung the quarters on the branch of a tree under which I lodged, and then I had to move for the bees and wasps were so thick about the fresh meat that I could not get near it.

From the Grand Mesa, which looks down on the Gunnison where it joins Grand River, I wandered down to Grand Junction, situated on the north bank of that stream in a sagebrush flat devoid of timber or shrubbery, another tent city, garnished with a multitude of wells with long wooden sweeps for raising water. This

UTE INDIANS ENCAMPED NEAR BEAR RIVER

Sketch by C. S. Stobie, First Scout, White River Ute Agency.

was before the railroad had been constructed down the Gunnison. I found the people very friendly and hospitable. They had high hopes of its development as a railroad center and of its agricultural and fruit possibilities because of a rich soil and favorable climate, combined with abundant water for irrigation. An immense valley, of which it seemed to be the center, was bounded on the north by high bluffs of upheaved strata of oil slate, beyond which the land sloped toward White River and embraced an excellent stock range, where the Utes pitched their tents and found easy hunting, for deer were very thick in those days.

From this point I drifted to the military camp on White River, where a battalion of the Fifth Infantry was in cantonment. Major Drum was in command and it was not long before I again became a scout for the government. My duties were light and I spent much time in hunting on the headwaters of White River. On the north fork, near the head of Bill Williams' Fork of Bear River, I found a beautiful little lake hidden in the forest, called Trappers' Lake, that was swarming with trout. There was not a sign of a trail leading to this lake, nor was there any grass for camping purposes.

To this spot I led a party of officers from the cantonment. There was no trail, so I took a straight course through the woods, crossing hills and ravines, and as we had a number of horses and pack animals a well-marked trail was left for those who came after.

It was a virgin trail, over new and out-of-the-way forest lands. Suddenly we came upon the residence of a beaver family; there was the dam across a little brook, with fresh-peeled willows and other edible-bark shrubbery scattered about. These clever rodents had selected, for safety, a site far from choice cottonwood saplings, their cherished food, and now they were no longer safe, for here was a trail! They were discovered at last. Their simple habitation of brush rose above water at one side of the dam and their pathways and slides lined the bank, the water still glistening where they had gamboled. Now all was discreet and still.

We passed along at a walk between the trees, when out of the forest sprang half a dozen wood deer with startled speed and away. We were now nearing Trappers' Lake and I had no time to play, for I was in the lead and wanted to strike the lake at its outlet, where the trout were so thick that they hid the shallow bottom. It was easy to miss, riding through the thick woods.

We had started one bright morning and instead of following the old wagon road that led to the forks of White River I cut to the left over the hills and we made an early camp in the timber where there was fine water and fresh game sign. After lunch I started off alone for fresh meat of some kind, either elk or deer, before the promiscuous shooting should frighten the game from the vicinity. In the evening or early morning I would have skirted the edge of the timber, but being midday I entered the wood and slowly and cautiously picked my way between the trees with all senses alert for signs and sounds, halting frequently to listen, for I sensed a game odor not far away. There did not seem to be a breath of air stirring for it was that hour after noon when all nature seems at rest.

Standing there, either by design or inadvertence I stepped on a dry twig, which snapped ever so lightly but occasioned a crash in the timber near by. I looked in the direction, but could see nothing but a white dead limb against a tree. As I looked, it moved in that stately and graceful fashion that strength gives to weight, and I knew it was a bull elk. The rest was easy. I fired and the elk lunged forward and dropped with a great tumult and thrashing of brush. With some difficulty I cleared a space sufficient to handle and dispose the animal for packing to camp. I returned at once to camp and had two of the soldiers saddle up and return with me for the meat and head.

The next morning we traveled down a long ridge to the north fork of White River and crossed; thenceforth it was through the forest until we reached the outlet of Trappers' Lake, where we stopped to rest and admire the swarm of trout that filled the stream at that point.

We found a little spot at the head of the lake where we might camp and have scant picking for the animals for at least one day and night. We made a pleasant camp in the open and caught with ease all the trout needful for our use and to take back to friends at the cantonment. These were exposed to the cold and frosty night air and in the morning wrapped in rushes.

I now led the party up a long ridge in the direction of Bill Williams' Fork of Bear River, where we camped in the pines. In the evening I went down the ridge a short distance and killed two black-tail deer, which were packed on the mules when we returned to the cantonment. We took with us, also, a hard-tack box which we had packed with trout in layers of leaves and green rushes in the frost of the early morning. Thus ended a very pleasant outing.

Some time after the excursion to Trappers' Lake, Captain Van Vliet and I spent a few days in the forested hills beyond the forks of White River, where deer and elk were plentiful. Once we stopped near the brink of a sharp ridge, where I peeped over and saw a buck reposing under a pine tree, and we watched that deer get to his feet carefully and almost crawl to cover, whence he bounded off to safety in the timber.

Another time while in the same neighborhood with Lieutenant Patterson we came upon the fresh trail of two bears in the early morning, when frost was on the grass. We followed it to the edge of the hill and peering over saw two bears, one brown and one black, standing at attention, listening with all their might. I fired at the big one, but the bullet drove high and made a splash on the ground beyond him.

With a single motion the bears turned and galloped up hill, coming straight in our direction. "Let's get to that tree!" I cried to the lieutenant, and we did, standing ready. Presently they came bounding along in their clumsy gait only a few yards away and when they were within thirty yards or less the officer fired at the big brown one and bruin dropped. The other one escaped. When we came to examine our prize we discovered that I had shot him through the ear.

One day the commanding officer sent for me and directed that I proceed to the camp of Colorow, and tell him to move out of the country. At that time his camp was somewhere on the head of Piceance Creek, and consisted of about a dozen lodges and tents. I had some trouble in finding the camp, but finally arrived in sight of it early in the evening.

Dismounting near the principal lodge and holding my horse by the lariat, I raised the canvas flap that served to cover the entrance and stepped within the smoky atmosphere. Several Indians were seated on skins and blankets in a circle about the fire, and a voice from one of them, whom I recognized as Colorow, greeted me with "How! How!"

"Colorow," I said, "the soldier chief at White River camp sent me to tell you that you must move your camp away from this White River country at once."

Colorow understood English fairly well. He was silent for a moment, then he said, "Well, where I go?"

"Follow the way water runs, the way the Utes went, across Green River into Utah," I told him.

"All right, all right, I go," he said, and made no further comment.

So the Indians had to move on. The region where they had pitched their tents was such as to give them a comfortable living, but apparently it was the policy of the Department of the Interior to assemble the Utes around the nearest agency, where they could be watched and taken care of. They would have been happier, I know, where they were not under the eyes of the military. The region they vacated was not made use of for years after their removal. I understand that in recent years oil shale has been found in it.

There being no feed in the vicinity nor any invitation for me to stay, I mounted my horse and took the back trail about five miles; then, turning off the trail into the hills, I found a comfortable place to spend the night, and picketing my horse, spread my blanket against the saddle and slept.

The next time I received orders they were given me in writing instead of verbally. It was the first week in October, 1882, when Major Drum issued an order from his camp on White River directing me to proceed on a scout over the trail leading southward to ascertain if there were any Indians about and to report upon its practicability as a wagon road. The scout was not to extend farther than Grand River.

I knew there were no Indians near the trail south to the Grand, so I took the trail west toward Piceance Creek in order to find out just where the Indians were and thus enable me to make a proper report. After proceeding some four or five miles on a plain trail in the *piñons,* I came face to face with a dozen Utes traveling in single file. The way was narrow, with rocks and trees on either side, and there was scarcely room to turn out. Clearly someone must get off the trail, and in that wild place the ethics in the premises might rest in point of numbers.

I kept on the trail until my horse's head touched the head of the horse bearing the leading Ute. We were all now at a standstill. The leader, a man of pleasant features, about twice my age, was simply habited in a leather shirt and had a black silk cloth around his head. We held a short confab, mostly in signs, in the course of which the leader learned that I was hunting, and I that they were on their way to the cantonment on some business whose nature I could not make out. Finally, the leader, reading my mind, perhaps, and realizing that I had no notion of giving them the road, pressed his bridle rein against the neck of his mount and with a smile turned off the path, the others following his example.

I pursued my journey without looking back. Late in the day I met a Ute riding in the direction I was going and joined him. In a couple of hours we came to his camp of several hundred people. I rode through the camp and returned to the trail I had left. I noted that very few people were outside of their tepees. I had got a few hundred yards away when I happened to look back and saw a multitude of armed Indians riding furiously in my direction.

I halted at once and waited their approach. They came on in a menacing attitude and I thought they were going to ride over me, but they checked their horses a few feet away and I suddenly found myself the center of a mob of gesticulating and excited Indians.

I made the sign that I did not understand and they brought forward a man who could talk English. He demanded to know what I was doing out there, and where the soldiers were. It was evident that the Indians supposed that I was spying out their camp.

"Tell your chief," I said to the interpreter, "that I met some of your people this morning on their way to the soldier camp on White River and they asked me the same question, and I told them that I was hunting and looking at the country. I am alone, and there are no soldiers anywhere except at their camp."

I rolled and lighted a cigarette and looked at my watch—not that I wanted to know the time of day, for I knew it was time to go. While they were debating among themselves I waved my hand with an "adios!" and passed on. I was doubtful whether I had convinced them that all was well, but they made no move to follow me and I rode until dark. Then, as on the previous occasion, I turned off the trail into the *piñon* hills, where I might find a place to sleep in safety.

Another incident occurred in the following winter. There were no thrills about it, only hard and drudging labor; the labor of following a mountain lion in deep snow.

"Yellowstone Kelly"

I had been looking for a band of elk whose tracks, a day or two old, showed along the foot of the mountains near Bill Williams' Fork, not far from the site of the Thornburg fight. While on their sign I ran onto the track of a mountain lion and followed it. Lions were common enough, but the track of this one was unusually large—the largest I ever ran across. Lions are cowardly creatures until wounded and cornered.

The snow was about a foot deep and the going rough, but I kept on to where the lion had stopped near a heavy bank of snow and excavated a pit nearly six feet in depth to the remains of a range steer incased in its shriveled hide. Satisfied that there was nothing there in the shape of food, the lion pursued his course and got into such rough country that it was too trying for my horse and I turned aside toward the lower country, for it was nearly dark and there was no place suitable for a camp. I had not gone more than a mile when I again ran on to his tracks, not more than twenty-four hours old and going in the direction of the starting point. I got off my horse and examined the track. It was the same old lion with the big feet, meandering toward the lower country where the deer flock along the juniper ridges, where there are rocky caverns and retreats.

Satisfied, I turned away from the lion's footprints, aiming to go far enough to be out of the scent of the beast, it being according to my experience a matter of chance or good luck to get within shot of such a wary prowler. I found a little bench where the horse could paw the snow and find short and succulent grasses and sweet herbage, which would hold him better than the dry, washed-out grass of the valley. I selected a spruce tree near by, under which I made my camp on the bare, dry ground.

I soon had a fire started and snow melting for coffee, there being no water anywhere near. I always carried meat tied to the saddle in starting out, for the reason that I might not want to shoot or lose time in hunting game; in any event I could take only a little of it and waste a whole lot. I usually carried ribs of deer or other game, which I roasted on the coals. So with a cup of coffee and roast ribs I could make out a satisfying meal without bread.

I placed my saddle at the trunk of the tree and rolled in the blanket and light canvas I carried. I was up by dawn and had breakfast, after which I picketed the horse, for I feared he might stray off in search of water, snow not being very satisfying. This hunt was to be afoot, and I lost no time in getting under way. I cut across to strike the track and when I got to it I found it looked much fresher in daylight. I began to feel there was a sporting chance to come up with him. The pursuit led me for hours up and down hill. Once I came to where the lion had maneuvered for position to pounce upon a deer. A bunch had been feeding on a hillside where there was scattered shrubbery that offered concealment. The outcome was plainly revealed, like a pictograph traced in the snow; how he crept from bush to bush, waiting patiently to make a further advance like a cat crawling on a bird or fowl; then, when close to the quarry, making a sudden dash which must have brought him very close to one deer, as shown by the scramble and springing of the surprised and frightened band as they scattered in flight, still pursued by the lion.

The tracks led to lower ground and I turned off the

direct trail to intercept it again in the direction I surmised they would go. When I again struck the trail of the deer there was no sign of the lion. By this time I was becoming weary of the chase, but I turned to the right and after traveling a mile had described a half circle before I again saw his fresh track. He was heading for higher ground and took a course that led toward camp. The way became rough, and in some rocky gulches he seemed uncertain which way to travel. Finally, as I topped a rock ridge to one side of the direct trail (I was beginning to be wary of him myself) and stopped to rest and look around, I saw him against some gray, shelving rocks about one hundred yards away. He was lying down looking straight at me.

I fired on the instant and he bounded into the air and disappeared over the ledge. I lost no time in making for the spot where I last saw him. There was blood on the rocks and his tracks led over another ridge, as I could see in the snow. When I had surmounted this point I saw him about fifty yards away, spitting and snarling, lying down and looking around in my direction. I let him have it again and he stretched out in the snow and when I got to him there was no sign of life.

He did not come up to my expectation in point of size, though far above the average, and his lower limbs and paws were abnormally large. A mountain lion that helped himself to one of our baits in the Judith Basin, Montana, was estimated to weigh one hundred and fifty to one hundred and sixty pounds. This animal would weigh more, and when the hide was stretched to dry later the legs were out of proportion, giving it an odd appearance.

Scouting in Colorado

I shall not weary the reader by describing my task of laying out a military route to the valley of Grand River, which was built by Captain Stephen Baker with two companies of infantry, nor the log cabin that I toiled to hew in one of the river loops in this same valley after the abandonment of the military cantonment on White River, which occurred a year or two later.

After the close of the military occupation in this region I was urged to proceed to some other station, but I preferred to remain in Colorado, where there were fine hunting grounds in the lands lately vacated by the turbulent Utes. Also, I had some notion of turning farmer, an idea which was destined never to materialize.

There was no longer any wild frontier on whose verge the picturesque savage disputed the passage of the white man. The campaigns conducted by General Miles against the allied Sioux and Cheyenne on their own domain, keeping the field regardless of the weather, alike in deep snow or in burning heat of midsummer, had convinced them of the futility of longer opposing the government. Strange to relate, many who had fought the whites most bitterly were among the first to adopt a peaceful mode of life and to turn their attention to the cultivation of the soil as a means of livelihood.

There was no longer in this region any field for the exercise of the talents of a scout, and my happy, eventful life on the plains drew to its close. My army friends found a place for me in the War Department and I returned once more to the peaceful life on which while still a mere boy I had turned my back. I was yet to wander far, to Alaska and the Philippines, and to undergo many interesting and venturesome experiences. But the recital of them must await another occasion. The present narrative properly ends with the termination of the happiest period of my life, as a plainsman and scout in the region of the Yellowstone.

INDEX

AMELIA POE, river steamboat, wrecked on upper Missouri, 89.

Arapaho Indians, hunting ground of, 213.

Arikara, shot at by Mike Welsh, 43-44; scalp Oglala shot by Kelly, 47-48; in hunting party, 87; peace treaty with Mandan and Hidatsa, 241.

Assiniboin, at Fort Buford, 52; bring pelts to Fort Peck, 58; meeting with, 63; on the road, 94; camp on Milk River, 183.

Atwood, Bill, rescues camp grindstone, 106-107.

BAILEY, Lieut. ——, secures ammunition, 91; examines ford, 157; forestalls Nez Percé raid on Carroll, 186.

Baird, Lieut. G. W., shot through the ear, 193; order signed by, 207.

Baker, Capt. Stephen, builds military route to Grand River Valley, 255.

Baldwin, Capt. ——, carries ammunition, 174; friendly tussle with Gen. Miles, 187.

Baldwin, Lieut. Frank D., attacks Sitting Bull's camp, 180; order signed by, 212.

Bannock Indians, Kelly ordered to report on, 212-213; captured by Gen. Miles, 223.

Barker, L., on trip down Yellowstone River in mackinaw, 176.

Bear eats grasshoppers in snowbank, 217-218.

Bear's Den Hill, life at, 13.

Bear's paw as a visiting card, 148.

Beaver, dried castors mixed with tobacco, 123; attempt to dig out, 129; construction of dam, "water farmer of the plains," 130; at McDonald's Creek, 134-135.

Bennett, Capt. ——, killed in fight with Bannock, 223.

Benteen, Capt. ——, in command of cavalry, 206.

Billy, half-breed scout, 154; interpreter, 158.

Blackfeet Indians, Judith Basin claimed by, 90; Bear Paw Mountain district claimed by, 108; war parties of, 117; Sioux wounded by, 143-144.

Bloody Knife, leader of Arikara hunting party, 44; scalps Sioux shot by Kelly, 47-48.

Blount, ——, corralled by Indians, 105.

Bowles, ——, partner of Major A. S. Reed, 117.

Index

Bread baked before camp fire, 16.

British commissioners to establish status of hostile Indians, 199; Kelly carries dispatches to, 201-203.

Broadwater, ——, owner of bull trains, 103.

Brughier, John, half-blood Sioux guide and interpreter, 158; joins Gen. Miles, escorts Cheyenne captives, 175; acquitted, 176.

Brule Indians, speech differs from Yankton, 92.

Bryant, Major ——, on Gen. Forsyth's staff, 99.

Buffalo Horn, Bannock scout, takes part in fight with Cheyenne, 167-172.

Buffaloes, used as wolf-bait, 61; attack hunters, 111, 113; method of cooking hump, 185.

Bull boats, made by Lambert and Kelly, 71, 73; method of propelling, 75-76.

Butler, Major ——, leads company against Cheyenne, 174.

CARROLL, town of, on Upper Missouri, 104; rendezvous for hunters and trappers, 105.

Carter, Capt. ——, in attack on Nez Percé, 193.

Casey, Major ——, leads company against Cheyenne, 174.

Chance, Lieut. ——, on Gen. Forsyth's staff, 99.

Chanda (tobacco), mixed with red willow bark, 56; given to Yankton, 182.

Chandopia, see *chanda.*

Chashasha (red willow bark), mixed with tobacco by Indians, 29, 49, 56, 181-182.

Cheyenne Indians, John Stanwix' experience with, 141; make peace with Gen. Miles, 153; tents arranged in circle, 154; women captured, 169; shot by Buffalo Horn, 172; medicine man dances along ridge, 174-175; captives escorted to camp, 175; assist Gen. Miles against Nez Percés, 189; lead advance, 192; in fight with Sioux, 232-239; Gen. Miles's campaigns against, 255.

Chippewa Indians, take Kelly across river in canoe, 17-18.

Clendenning, ——, trader at Carroll, 136.

Colorow, offers two horses for Kelly's rifle, 241; murders Meeker, Ute agent, 243; ordered to leave White River country, 248-249.

Cooley, George, cook at Fort Peck, 153.

Cooper, Jim, a Georgian at Carroll, 105.

Coyotes, of little commercial

Index

Index

Index

in hunting party, 87; unearth cache made by Nez Percés, 205.

HADDO, Corporal ——, on scout with Kelly and Welsh, 180-184; on scout with Kelly and Tripp, 189-192; killed, 195.

Half-breeds, Kelly joins party of, to make pemmican, 19-23.

Hall, Capt. Robert, battalion commander, 4.

Hargous, Lieut. ——, leads detachment in fight with Cheyenne, 171.

Harvest festival, Indian, 29.

Heintzelman, Capt. ——, post quartermaster, 207.

Hidatsa Indians, peace treaty with Arikara and Mandan, 241.

Horn, George, goes wolf-hunting with Sandy Morris, 108; killed by Santee, 109.

Howard, Gen. O. O., campaign against Nez Percés, 184, 186, 215-216; consults Gen. Miles, 198.

Howard, John, accompanies Kelly on trip to the Missouri, 184.

Hump, Indian scout, kills Nez Percé, 193-194; is wounded, 195.

Hunkpapa Indians, cross Big Dry with pelts, 57; control buffalo range, 149.

INDIAN, method of making pemmican, 22; burial ground, 25; village, 27-29; harvest festival, 29; initiation of warriors, 29; sweat bath, 30; "mulligan," 34-35; etiquette, 48; pipe ceremonial, 49, 122-123; dance, 51-52; manners, 121-122; pipe-bearer, 123.

JACK, Ute chief, leads attack against cavalry commanded by Major Thornburg, 242-244.

Jerome, Lieut. ——, goes as hostage to Nez Percé camp, 198.

"Johnson, Liver-eating," hunter and frontiersman, on Tongue River expedition, 167.

Johnsons, the three, scouts on Tongue River expedition, 167.

Jones, Capt. ——, takes direct route to geyser basin, 221.

Joseph, Chief, taken to United States under guard, 150; surrenders at Bear Paw Mountains, 180; leads Nez Percé retreat, 185-198; trapped by U. S. troops, 193; asks for parley, surrenders, 198.

KELLY, Luther S., in Civil War, 2-6; at Fort Wadsworth, 7-12; at Bear's Den Hill, 13-14; at Fort Garry, 17; joins party of Red River half-breeds, 19-23; meets Sit-

261

Index

ting Bull, 20-21; at Fort Berthold, 25-31; carries mail from Fort Buford to Fort Stevenson, 40-44; duel with two Oglala, 45-47; at Fort Buford, 49-53; at Fort Peck, 57-58; trapping and hunting, 58-66; explores Yellowstone with Ed Lambert, 67-76; encounter with war party, 81-83; goes hunting with Indians, 85-88; in Milk River country, 89-93; meets party of Yankton, 91-93; recovers horse from Fort Berthold Indians, 95-97; accompanies Gen. Forsyth up the Yellowstone on *Far West,* 98-102; guides Broadwater's bull train, 103-104; at Carroll, 104-109; goes to Bear Paw Mountains with Sandy Morris, 109-112; encounter with Yankton raiders, 114-116; goes wolf-hunting with Mike Welsh and Erwin brothers, 118-136; joins John Stanwix, 140-146; reports to Gen. Miles at Powder River, 148; is sent to Milk River country, 149-153; makes night march on trail of Cheyenne, 154-156; accompanies Gen. Miles on winter campaign, 160-175; takes trip to New York and Washington, 177; travels with Two Moons, 177-179; goes north to look for hostile Indians, 180-183; on scouting trips during Nez Percé retreat, 184-198; carries dispatches to Gen. Terry, 199-203; recovers Gen. Miles's saddle horse, 205-206; goes from Fort Keogh to Deadwood, 206-211; scouting trips in Yellowstone Park, 212-228; joins hunting party from Fort Keogh, 229-230; follows Sioux who had attacked Sandy Morris, 232-239; goes to military camp on White River, 245; sends Colorow to Utah, 248-249; encounters Utes, 250-251; shoots mountain lion, 252-254; lays out military route to valley of Grand River, 255; obtains place in War Department, 255; goes to Alaska and Philippines, 255.

LaFARGE, Tom, interpreter for the Crows, on Tongue River expedition, 167; horse shot, 170.

Lambert (Lambier), Ed, Canadian voyageur and post interpreter at Fort Buford, 50-51; cautions Kelly, 54; explores Yellowstone with Kelly, 67-76.

Larb, mixed with tobacco, 42, 63-64; dried castors of beaver mixed with, 123.

Leavitt, Private ——, 207-211,

Index

Index

232; result of campaigns conducted by, 255.

Milford, George, at Fort Berthold in 1868, 31.

Minnesota, volunteer cavalry return, 9.

"Missouri," trapper, joins Kelly's hunting party, 80; in fights with Indians, 81-83.

Morris, Sandy, encounters with Sioux, 108-109, 114-116, 230-231; hunting trips with Kelly to Bear Paw Mountains, 109-112; joins party in pursuit of Sioux, 232.

Mountain lion, strikes down Indian warrior, 137; killed by Kelly, 252-254.

NEWCOMB, Tom, scout, accompanies Kelly on trip with dispatches for Gen. Terry, 199-205.

Nez Percé Indians, retreat of, 91; sent to United States under guard, 150; retreat before Gen. Howard's forces, 184; elude Seventh Cavalry near Heart Mountain, 186; cross river below Cow Island, 187; surrounded by Gen. Miles, 192-193; surrender to Gen. Miles, 198; cache of captured freight unearthed by Grosventres, 205; removed to Indian Territory, 206; account of retreat, 215-216.

Norris, Bill, visits camp of Broadwater's bull train, 104; brings Kelly message from Gen. Miles, 186.

Norris, ——, superintendent of Yellowstone Park, headquarters at Mammoth Hot Springs, 222; sends Kelly to meet cavalry troop, 224; builds roadway along trail, 228; road of glass, 228-229.

Northwest Mounted Police, outpost encountered, 202.

OGLALA Indians, Kelly's duel with, 45-47; at Fort Buford, 51-52; cross Big Dry with pelts, 57; meet Lambert and Kelly, 72-73; speech differs from Yankton, 92; control buffalo range, 149.

Okshena Duta, burial place of, 58-59.

Otis, Col. ——, in command of station on lower Yellowstone, 150; tells of attack on wagon train, 153.

PARSHALL, George, mail-carrier between Fort Buford and Fort Stevenson, long overdue, 40; returned, 50.

Patterson, Lieut. ——, with Kelly in White River country, 248.

Pawnee Indians, Newcomb mistakes Grosventres for, 204.

Pease, Mag, Mandan Indian in winter camp, 33.

Index

Index

Reed's Cabin, 135-136; Stanwix' experience with, 141-144; Gen. Crook follows, 146; make peace with Gen. Miles, 153; Gen. Miles plans winter campaign against, 160; camped on Frenchman's Creek, 183; return after raid for Crow horses, 185; organized as auxiliary force against Nez Percés, 189; lead advance, 192; rumor of plan to assist Nez Percés, 197; suffer from cold and hunger, 229; attack Sandy Morris and his partner, 230-231; pursued by cavalry, Kelly, Morris, and Cheyenne scouts, 232-234; kill Douglass, wound cavalryman, 235; scout volunteers to carry dispatch to post, 235-236; surrender, 239; Gen. Miles's campaigns against, 255.

Sitting Bull, visits camp on Mouse River; meets Kelly, 20-21; frequents buffalo ranges between the Yellowstone and the Missouri, 70; shows white men how to trade with Indians, 71; nearly captured by Lieut. Baldwin, 180; rumor of plan to assist Nez Percés, 197; joint commission to establish status of, 199; refuses to attend council if soldiers are present, 203; followers suffer from cold and hunger, 229; capture of Sioux from camp of, 239; believed to be in Canada, 240.

Smith, Vic, scout, at Powder River, 146; conversation with Gen. Miles, 148-149; accompanies Kelly on scout to Milk River country, 150-153.

Snyder, Capt. ——, sends White Bull to parley with Sioux, 238.

Stanwix, John, with party of trappers and prospectors, joined by Kelly, 140; experience with war party of Sioux and Cheyenne, 141-144; bound for the upper Yellowstone, 145-146.

Stony Indians, on hunting expedition, 112-113.

Sturgis, Gen. ——, eluded by Nez Percés, 215-216.

Sun of the Star, Indian chief, accompanies Gen. Miles to Fort Berthold, 31.

TERRY, Gen. Alfred H., meets British commissioners, 199; Kelly and Newcomb report to, 200; sends Kelly and Newcomb to border, 201; leaves camp for border, 203.

Teton Indians, at Fort Buford, 51; bring pelts to Fort Peck, 57; accent differs from that of Assiniboin, 63; on upper reaches of the Missouri,

266

Index

Index

bring pelts to Fort Peck, 57; accent differs from that of Assiniboin, 63; Kelly meets party of, 91-93; control buffalo range, 149; Kelly gives tobacco to, 182; dialect generally used in region of the upper Missouri, 234.

Yellow Bull, Cheyenne scout, in pursuit of Sioux, 233-234.